I0099104

Healed, Survived

Perfect Message

DERRICK R. HARDING

Copyright © 2018 Derrick Harding

ISBN:

All rights reserved. No part of this publication may be reproduced, stored in a retrieval system, or transmitted in any form or by any means - electronic, mechanical, photocopy, recording, scanning, or other – except for brief quotations in critical reviews or articles, without the prior written permission of the publisher.

Printed in New York by:

OMNIBOOK CO.
99 Wall Street, Suite 118
New York, NY 10005
USA
+1 202-738-1322
www.omnibookcompany.com

First Edition

For e-book purchase: Kindle on Amazon, Barnes and Noble
Book purchase: Amazon.com, Barnes & Noble, and www. omnibookcompany.com
Omnibook titles may be purchased in bulk for educational, business, fund-raising, or sales promotional use. For more information please e-mail

Acknowledgment

FIRST, I Must RECOGNIZE the sovereignty of God in my life for rescuing me from condemnation. I was a wretched sinner condemned to die but through God's providence I'm alive. On the other hand, I still cannot reconcile the fact that he's given me the privilege of carrying this sickness in my body, miraculously healed and now put words in my mouth to declare his goodness.

But I must give oodles of appreciation to several significant persons. First, my darling wife Shelly. She extended the hand of God as my help mate. Then to the brethren at the Fire who kept the prayer vigil going. Thanks to my Bishop and his wife, for remembering me financially and in their prayers; to my brother Kent who blessed me financially as well. Then thanks brother Neville my donor, who unselfishly mortgaged his stem cells, to give me new bone marrow. and his wife who stood beside and with him all the way. Also, my siblings Tyrone, Norma and Joan who tested to see if they were suitable match to be my donor. God bless you; Yet I cannot forget my care giver Pauline who worked tirelessly to help me with my diet and medication.

To all the folks at Palm Spring and Fair Prospect Hospital's Bone Marrow Center, you blessed me, and I bless you back.

And to my brothers, Stokes, and Monty, Dennis and Aston; who were my drivers, meal carriers, and prayer partners. You never let me down. I cannot forget the cooks who sent me dinner. Then I must thank my local editors: Dr. Castle, and Mrs. Stacy Ramos. Thank you all for working with me to make my dream come to fruition. Now thank God, the past is over. God has given me another chance at life. "I know that everything God does will remain forever; there is nothing to add and there is nothing to take from it, for God has so worked that men should fear Him. (ESV Ecclesiastics

1

Sunday February 16, 2014, every nerve fiber in my body work at optimum capacity. I enjoyed a state of wholeness of physical, social, emotional and psychological well-being. O yes, I felt thankful to be alive. My mind, body, soul and spirit experienced an effervescence of unrestrained energy. This positive mind set, propelled me into my morning's agenda. Therefore, I pay homage to my Lord and Savior who kept me during the night.

Derrick Harding, 68 years old, a school teacher for over thirty years, was a picture of health and vigor. He is a short five feet six-inches-tall man, who weighed one hundred and forty -seven pounds and vowed to keep it that way. He is the ninth child of Ethel and David Harding, avowed Evangelic Christians, farmer and house wife. He was not exposed to the world until, he was admitted into teacher training college.

Up early that morning, brimming with energy, "I, exude faith in the divine power of the Almighty, that makes me feel as tall as the tallest man alive."

Subsequently, I took command of the day to bring my faith in alignment with the fullness of His many blessings, through His providence of supplying all things according to His riches in glory by Christ Jesus." Philippians 4:19. As such, I set forth to chart a course on this beautiful divinely-anointed day with daily devotion. Next, I broke into my number one exercise routine, running gracefully on the spot. This, I fondly called Zimzum, complement of a tradition I adopted from a brilliant little old man with a giant spirit. My mother cared for him and called him Maas Eddy, when I was a boy. He was affectionately called Mass Eddy because of his short stature and his huge head and brilliant mind. He would run and dance on the spot and chant "Zimzum, Zimzum," which he intellectually expressed with clarity, as he characterized himself as having performed with vim and vivacity. He always carried himself with a certain air of noble posture complement to his lean, trim, body and upright gait. Thus, I chanted and moved in his style, gracefully, in place with effortless motion. I glided like the silky, smooth, rhythmic tapping of a ballpoint font from an electric typewriter, preserving words of romance and life experiences. I closed my eyes as I enjoyed the aura of divine peace.

This beauty and peace of the sunlight shone in all its glory that Sunday morning and suggested nothing sinister, nothing dull, nothing broken, nothing lacking, but all according to the master's will, full of grace and excitement. It ensured all the features that were reflective of a gorgeous and lovely day.

The February winter gust, with radiating temperatures of seventy-nine degrees, accompanied by my body heat generated from this treasured routine was just perfect. It contributed not to a feeling of fear, but to a spirit of power and love and a sound mind. I thought of nothing else but to join the folks at the Fire, to worship the Son of Righteousness. Thus, deservedly, I was ushered into the shower, singing loudly: "*There is sunshine in my soul today, More glorious and bright. Than glows in any earthly sky, For Jesus is my light. O there's sunshine, blessed sunshine, While the peaceful, happy moments roll; When Jesus shows His smiling face. There is sunshine in my soul*"

With this state of mind, my body, in sync, tempered by the mornings mild 75 degrees, my daily routine and the surrounding pleasant atmosphere, complement of Psalm 19:1 (KVJ) "The heavens declare the glory of God; And the firmament shows his handiwork," there was neither signs nor symptoms of health issues. I was, so it seemed, in the best shape of my life.

Yet, at church that morning, one man prayed for me against an imminent bone marrow disease. Unmistakably, and without warning, my life took on a new meaning. The characteristics emanated, from that time forward, placed a demand on everything I did. I was destined to trust God on a new level. Life had become more urgent. I walked more briskly and did everything on time. I carefully practiced the saying "Do not put off what you can do today for tomorrow." I seemed to turn my thoughts inward rather than looking outwardly. Life became purposeful. My only regret is that I have not continued that same path.

The radiant sun outside my home church, the Fire Worship Center showed no contrasting wave from the Spirit that radiated joyfully on the faces of the believers who worshipped inside. They clapped and enthusiastically clattered tambourines in rhythm to the glorious sound of music, followed by a lusty "Praise the Lord." Yet the day was absent of drama, except the forecasting of what was in my divine menu. There was the usual excellent singing by the praise team, creative announcements, dance by Whispers of Praise and birthday surprises, that were bound to make us laugh. Then for the climax, the bishop gave a rousing, spirit-filled sermon and prayer. Bishop, a forceful man, five feet five inches tall, with broad shoulders and a loud voice, founded the church thirty-nine years ago. He's married and has three biological children, one adopted and eight adorable grandchildren. He is an A type personality and a strong business man via which he plies his trade in teaching business to young entrepreneurs and businessmen

Subsequently, those who needed healing were ministered to by prayer and "laying on of hands." Those who needed to bolster their faith waited anxiously for an extra word from the bishop, while the rest of the audience filed out nonchalantly. On the contrary, a fellow elder and my best friend walked to the front of the sanctuary.

He was a baker by trade and a devoted Family Man. He was a thin lean man, five feet three inches tall with a full head of grey hair. I looked in his face and saw that his eyes had a yellowish-brown and watery appearance. His countenance was solemn, and he had a concerned. "Your eyes look very pale and watery," I said. "May I pray for you?" Willingly, he knelt in compliance. I laid my hand on his head and prayed that our Father would revitalize his spirit and heal every ailment in his body.

In turn, he said with the deepest conviction, "The Holy Spirit says that I'm to pray for your bone marrow." I shivered as he got set to pray for me. He clasped both of palms around my knees, bowed his head, and prayed, among other things, "Father, give my brother a new bone marrow." Oblivious that he was prophesying the future of my life, he set in motion a catalyst that would change the course of my life. He rose, we shook hands and thank each other and departed.

One day later, I was diagnosed with a bone marrow disease. Right away I knew that I'd be healed of the disease, leukemia, because I'd the right perspective of the divine power of healing.

This wasn't the only mind-boggling experience that created confidence and absolute assurance in me. It had caused me to declare my healing even before treatment commenced. This reminds me of the verse: "Before you call He answers, while you are yet speaking He hears." (Isaiah 65:24) There were other convincing instances that supported my audacious authority. I firmly believed that not only would I beat the malady that attacked my immune system, but that my Father would give me a platform to glorify His name.

Similarly, one Sunday my Bishop, his wife, their armor bearers, and a few members of the Fire Worship Center went to Dallas, Texas, for fellowship. During the service, the officiating minister paused and asked for the person who had a bone marrow disease. Nobody else responded but those from the Fire Worship Center. Although I wasn't present in body, my brethren reported on my condition, and one of my fellow elders stood in proxy for me, leading the minister to pray for my healing.

Likewise, I'd just entered Palm Hospital where I started chemotherapy during the first weeks of hospitalization. There, I was visited by a couple whose son had been healed of leukemia. The tall lady, who acted as the spokesperson, was authoritative, but soft spoken. She seemed to be in the fifty- age bracket. She towered over my bed, as she declared that The Father would heal me as he did their son. At the end of the prayer, she encouraged me to be strong and to put my faith and trust in God. Then the she gave me a card with words inscribed on both sides. On one was: "God Bless You" written in decorative colors and the other, *"This affliction will not come back' (Nahum 1:9)."* I accepted this, and the other experiences as described above, and I decisively declared my healing.

Consequently, I was so moved during the early months in the hospital that I found myself to be an encourager of people rather than a recipient, of encouragement. It broke my heart to hear some cried. A couple of my colleagues called me from my workplace. They could hardly finish their statement of wishing me a speedy recovery before they burst into tears. I led some in prayer and encouraged others to know that this sickness wasn't unto death but to give glory to The Lord. He was giving me a platform to give glory to His name, I told them.

Two of my brothers literally crumbled in despondence and shed grievous tears. One brother called me one night. He explained, "Derrick, my heart is weak. I can't bear to hear you talk like that. When I look at your eyes and see your features, watch you walk and stumble, and you say that you are healed, it makes no sense to me. The problem is that you don't realize how sick you are." he said. He too broke in tears. He was right to some extent. On my hospital chart that the doctor wrote was his scientific knowledge. He was right on this account. That science was right in all human terms. Yet what was written in my Father's book was spiritual. "Daughter, (son), your faith has healed you. Go in peace and be freed from your suffering." "The view of the human body as a machine and of the mind as a separate entity is being replaced by one that sees not only the brain, but also the immune system, the bodily organs, and even each cell as a living, cognitive system." As a result, there are several machines that are programmed to respond to the human machine to pinpoint with great accuracy the effect of some malady. Yet the Father of all creation in His word said, "Do not despise small beginnings." (Zachariah 4:10) Faith as a grain of mustard seed is very small but when applied it removes the most stubborn ailment. He created man, gave him knowledge and wisdom to create and manage the practice of medicine, so man's wisdom is limited and subjected to God's wisdom which is passed finding out. "Just as the heavens are higher than the earth, so my ways are higher than your ways, and my thoughts are higher than your thoughts" (Isaiah 55:9). What he creates He can repair. He repairs with faith by his word. He was wounded for our transgression, He was bruised for our iniquity the chastisement of our peace was upon Him and by His stripes we are healed. On the other hand, scientist recommend physical medication which is most harmful. I got a medication from my Cardiologist called Tramadol which has over one hundred side effects. God performed one surgery, when he put Adam to sleep and removed his rid to form Eve. Today surgeons perform surges every day. I would go for the spiritual, none invasive, or invasive surgery any day.

My brother couldn't understand the working of faith by the word of God. For faith is the substance of things hoped for, the evidence of things not seen. He needed to see physical outward signs to believe. This was the experience of Thomas. Until Jesus showed him his wounds he didn't believe. My getting a good night's sleep my brother said, was predicated on knowing that you are well before I go to bed." "Please sleep in confidence, my brother, and have sweet dreams," I replied. "You aren't to worry. The Lord has healed me." I could imagine his bid round face and brown eyes streaming tears. In the past, he would reach for a bottle and poured himself a strong drink to calm his nerves, but age and wisdom had saved this brilliant, retired police officer from the fate of the bottle. He obviously didn't share my joy.

You may call these reports coincidence or providence, whichever you choose, but I believe that the people involved, who prayed for me heard from the Lord, while the others failed to believe in divine healing.

As a result, on February 17, without reservation, I kept an appointment that I'd made to see a hematologist, who sent me to do an ultrasound. He was a man whose width make him look shorter than the five feet eight inches tall that he was. He had fair complexion and thrived in his late fifties to early sixties. He was sort of a tired-looking and weighed seemed to weigh one hundred and seventy pounds. He was dressed in white shirt and tie covered by a white overcoat. His room was simply decorated but with elegant paintings on the wall. He'd a computer on his desk that answered his questions. Also, a printer nearby, which he used to print out my information. He also had other medical accessories in addition to two filing cabinets from which he retrieved and stocked files in my presence.

My visit to his office was tainted with mixed feelings. On the one hand, I was pleased to finally get words about my blood counts, and on the other, it came as unpleasant news. In his response to me, the hematologist said that he found negative traces in my blood, which were consistent with unhealthy bone marrow. Consequently, he sent the sample back to the lab for further verification and told me he would contact me later.

My wife accompanied me to his office that day. We left his office nearly noon. On our way, dropped by at Friday's restaurant for lunch. The place was sparsely crowded, just the usual midday crowd.

We enjoyed a meal and went home and had a good night's sleep. Then as usual, I prepared for school the next day and went early.

Without any excitement, usual fights, or calling on the public-address system for students to report to the main office, I performed my usually enjoyable and natural functions as a teacher. I didn't give a thought to what the doctor had said. Concentrating on my days actives, I didn't express concern for what the doctor said. I finished my duties for the day and headed to the gymnasium for my usual workout. I was rather nonchalant that evening. I didn't find Mac, Jose or Bob. Loneness didn't phase, me rather, it caused me to I concentrate better. When I turned on the music and got into my routines I forgot that I was the solitary occupant of the gymnasium.

At 7:00 p.m., I was enjoying the euphoria of my timely exercises, workout. The clock on the gym wall seemed to care, it struck. I looked. A small voice nudged at me. "Go home."

Immediately, I obeyed. I got dressed, drew the door shut, and headed for home. A scant thirty minutes elapsed, and I was alighted from my red 2007 Toyota motor car and made entrance to the confines of my home. Suddenly, the telephone interrupted the comfort of what was supposed to be a relaxing evening. With reluctance, I strode to its desk, still slinging my schoolbag over my left shoulder. Oops! Before I picked up the receiver, the ringing stopped. I shrugged my shoulders and put down my bag. Just then the telephone rang again. This time I reached for the receiver and heard, "Mr. Harding, did you know that you should report to Palm Hospital to be admitted?"

"Admitted?" he inquired.

"Yes, sir," the pleasant voice responded. "Do you mind if I put you on hold for a few minutes?"

"No, no," I replied, anxious to hear the reason. In the mean while I twiglet my fingers. I sat up erect at the edge of the chair. Having not found a more relaxing position, I held on to the chair seat with both hands.

The next voice brought what should've been the most devastating news. It brought back a whole new perspective to my life. What the hematologist told me and the prayer my friend prayed at the Fire, were both manifested as a reality.

"Mr. Harding, good evening;" the very tired voice that had been speaking throughout the long day, speculating over one diagnosis after the other, continued. "I am afraid I don't have very good news for you. You have leukemia."

"Leukemia?" I asked.

"Yes, sir, it's a blood disease. It's very difficult to manage, but it's curable," he said in a matter-of-fact voice, probably so, as to prevent greater discouragement my fainting heart, or dropping the receiver, I suppose. "But you'll have a good doctor," he continued.

"This is to glorify God," I said.

He didn't reply but proceeded to give me instructions to find my way to the hospital. "Everything would be prepared for you. When you get there, take the elevator to the third- floor and you will be told what to do," he said, and I pondered his instructions.

2

I LINGERED AND WALKED AIMLESSLY AROUND the house, not able to wrap my mind around this unbelievable diagnosis. I remained speechless. I shoved my hands in my pocket I sat on the edge of the settee. It didn't make sense. The horrifying news kept swirling around in my head. My heart didn't race, nor did I cry. I reserved my response. I really surprised myself at the way I remained calm even though I should've been awestruck about this diagnosis. Man, this was the shock of my life, but it reminds me of the scripture "Thou will keep him in perfect peace, whose mind is stayed on thee: because he trusts in You." (Isaiah 26 :3)

My darling wife, Shelly, came home, and I broke the news to her as gently as I could, but she just didn't know what to say, so she stared at me with a quizzical look. Shelly was always a calm supportive wife. She was fifty- five years old then and carried her five feet three inches height and one twenty-five pounds very well. She is a teacher by profession, a very good one, and devoted Christian. She was dedicated to her students, and daily we shared the of heart of her Kindergarten spirit. She loves spending Saturdays at the Pembroke Lakes Mall. She had her hair weaved that night and rolled up in a bun. She removed the band and let down heir. We made the decision and joined forces. We positively decided, with no other choice, but to carry out the instructions the hematologist gave me.

As appropriately, we packed only a few necessities in a small bag. Then we set out for the hospital. On our way, we didn't talk much. We just kept each other's spirit alive by singing spiritual songs that we learned from church. I believe one of the songs we sang was this:

Jesus took my burden and left me with a song.

My anxious fear subsided, my spirit was made strong;
Jesus took my burden and left me with a song.

We never cried, laughed or showed real sadness; we were rather in a pensive mood.

Jesus did take my burden because He knew I couldn't bear it alone. That is why Isaiah 53:4 says, "*Surely, he has borne our grief*, *and carried our sorrows*," because His father asked Him to carry our laid our sins. Acting on the doctor's instructions, we arrived about 8:30 p.m., only to be awed when we saw these imposing high-rise edifices with their bright lights, making the place looked like a perfect day. This was Palm Hospital. The occasion was foreboding. It wasn't easy to come to terms with my fate, not knowing how or when I'd return home again. There were hundreds of motor vehicles dazzling in the light in the parking lots, which made the hospital seem even bigger, if you consider the large number of people who occupants of the cars represented.

We drove under the covered two-lane entrance and parked. I waited for Shel. to drive the car to a convenient parking space. Then, without trepidation, we entered the elevator and rode together to the third floor. This was Western End, the bone marrow center. Like the hematologist said, everything was prepared. I paused at the desk, the nursing station, and politely introduced myself. The nurse on duty stared straight at me and I said: "Good evening, I'm

Mr. Harding. This is my wife, Shelly." She greeted us with a soft handshake and an elegant smile.

"Mr. Harding, we were expecting you," she spoke politely. One of the nurses at the dark-spotted semi-brown-curved granite top desk responded.

"Please go to room 3787," she continued.

This room became mine for the next months and three other subsequent times when I returned for chemotherapy treatment.

The first thing that impressed me about my place of comfort was the air-conditioning. Room 3787, as all the other rooms, was conveniently equipped with its own air-conditioning system controlled by automatic built-in thermostat. Therefore, I was privileged to regulate the temperature and adjust it to my liking. This just served to support the thought that I was absent from my home, but I could feel safe where I was. It was a perfect scenario. It was to me the real deal. It was rare, as it was important, because the illness that grievously attacked me, leukemia, generates low platelets and low white blood cell counts, which automatically would, reduce my resistance to cold temperature.

Unfortunately, though, the system malfunctioned, and I suffered unbearable cold from this discomfort. My sinusitis flared-up suddenly, and the left side of my face became swollen and numb like it had cocaine injected in it for a tooth removal. I reported the matter to my oncologist and his team, adjusted my bed so that I wasn't exactly under the vent. This helped somewhat, but the entire room was so cold it only added sweet sorrow. I'd cover my head under the sheet all day and repeated that at nights. However, I made one phone call to the maintenance department, which brought into action the efficient service of a truly reliable and capable technician. He came and adjusted it the same day. I responded with gratitude in writing, expressing special sentiments of thanks on my own business card.

Subsequently, as expected, I turned up the thermostat to the maximum eighty-five degrees, which gave me warmth and absolute comfort. On the contrary, when nurses who attended to my needs, came into the room, they complained that they were burning up while I was free from cold.

Then the next thing that impressed me, was the whole decor. The wooden floor was specially designed and cleaned and polished daily to accommodate patients and facilitate their living in healthy, germ-free surroundings. Everything seemed to be perfect.

I had never been hospitalized before. Therefore, Palm Hospital was simply a wonder to me. My first impression about the accommodation and beauty of the facility was "Wow." It was simply a beautiful facility. Room 3787, overlooked Richmond County, allowing me to appreciate the wonderful, picturesque view of the southern sky. The room and the scene were unimaginable just like pictures of a Hollywood movie. You could see the hand of Creator at work. You could see that the room was fitted just for patients like me. When I saw it, I knew that I couldn't die in there, not with all the state-of-the-art equipment in place, prepared to give me the best treatment possible.

It really humbled me to see how the Father of lights watched out for me. Since I didn't know what to expect, it just made me feel very small in the hands of a big, magnificent divine Almighty. Indeed, "It is, He Who ultimately rules the affairs of men." He made preparation to promote me. Therefore, I realized the plan and purpose of Him who called me from darkness into His marvelous light. (1 Peter 3. 1). This was business between me and the Holy one the "Ancient of Days" It had to become public, knowledge and I was the chosen vessel to hear, absorb and bring it to life: "Christ in me the hope of glory." ("Colossians 1:27"). The hope of glory, I believed that I was privileged to be chosen to do was this awesome demonstration of faith.

Then, to add real assurance to my liking the room, before I rolled down the window blinds at nights, I could observe with gratitude the whole panorama of the southern lights of the city, as they glittered brightly. When I awoke in the mornings, the burst of the glorious sunrise welcomed me. It was totally in contrast of the night's bewilderment, emphasizing the word that "weeping may endure for a night, but joy comes in the morning" (Psalm 30:5).

It was with a sense of hope, joy, and absolute pleasure to wake up and behold the beauty and majesty of the Creator, who sustained me in my right mind. To read the obituary column of the Newspaper each passing day, it was obvious that my name was not enlisted. It was an absolute blessing. My death could've been numbered in the reports, "but He who is, rich in mercies, (Ephesians 2:4) sustained me.

From my view also, I witnessed the wonders in the changes of the mystery of the morning's weather. This was a prerequisite to the breathtaking glories of the afternoon, as they by design, bid farewell to each other, though opposites, they revealed no rancor. The radiance of the sunlight had no darkness to dim its light. Yet subsequently, mystery unfolded. Dark cumulous clouds like puffy pieces of floating cotton swirled unhurriedly across the sky. Then thunder— loud, majestic rumble that streaked its breathtaking scenic swipes of lightning, briefly and periodically created a home décor tapestry that brings more mystery to the already lovely day. Additionally, sunlight and rain mingled in sweet harmony to create one of the paradoxes of nature: "the sun was shining, and rain was falling. This could only have been the touch of the master's hand. Then came a rainbow of assurance as His word that said: I do set my rainbow in the cloud, and it shall be for a token of a covenant between me and the earth. (Geneses 9:13)

All too soon, a pleasant afternoon was perfected in color, warmth, and culminating activities. Birds and other animals move to their place of rest. The skies at the last bad farewell to the setting sun. Presently, above, the east–west wind current piloted a small f lock of white birds with yellow feet and red beaks, confirming the wonder of the Savior's touch of majesty, as they moved in isosceles formation and perfect congruence. Guided by His divine hand, they winged their way effortlessly westward across the dark orange-colored sky to their natural sanctuary, secured by natural design, to calm them from the restless toil of their busy day.

Above and below me you could hear doors opening and slamming and the conversational tones in the good-byes as workers left for the day. Down in the courtyard, cars positioned themselves in line at the stoplight leading from the hospital parking lot. All, observed the no-noise protocol. They filed with flickering taillights as they awaited their turn, then filed slowly out through the gate, like a funeral procession.

Likewise, on my hospital bed, I craved with certainty the calming presence of my Savior's hand to maintain my stability after a day of restlessness. It would be vain for me to rise early and stay up late, toiling to sustain myself, when the scriptures states that, He grants sleep to his beloved (Psalm 127:2).

I lay on my back, my head covered, tears streaming down the sides of my face then popping in my ears. I did this not because I was sad, not because I was afraid or lonely, though often I was, but because I was engulfed by the grace and mercy of my Lord and Savior. I felt the hush of His comfort so the bit of discomfort, but not pain, perhaps, made me a little weary, as I ref elected on the goodness of my Savior. This prompted me to quote the reliable, time-tested, and all-appealing verse of scripture:

> *The heavens declare the glory of God and the firmament shows His handy work; Day unto Day utters speech and night unto night shows knowledge.*
> *There is no speech nor language where their voice is not heard.* (Psalm 19:1–3)

This most awesome experience pleased my musical taste buds and evoked a song I love as I blessed Him for keeping me alive. The sound of the melody came with effusive rapport from my lips. I filled my sixty- eight-year-old lungs with air and let loose the gift of life. I couldn't help but celebrate the wonder and majesty of my divine Mentor as I sang,

> *All things bright and beautiful; All creatures great and small, all things wise and wonderful the Lord God made them all; He gave us eyes to see them*
> *And lips that we might tell; how great is God almighty, who has made all things well.*

3

CONSEQUENTLY, ON THAT, AUSPICIOUS TUESDAY night, February 18, nurses came into my room to welcome me joyfully and to start me on what seemed to have been a never-ending journey to my miraculous recovery. They were never in a hurry but paced themselves efficiently, so it seemed. Being oblivious to the magnitude of this journey, they alleviated my misunderstandings by making me feel that I was the most important person in the world. They prepared me for my first procedure, an ultrasound. Preparation entailed my drinking four cups of some red dye mixed in my choice of juice, cranberry. One, with not so pleasant a taste, was gulped down every forty-five minutes. I started about 9:45 p.m. and finished about 12:45 a.m. Having satisfactorily completed the ingesting the drink, I was wheeled on my bed, which became my official limousine, to the radiology lab for the procedure.

The journey to the lab was down a long hallway. I made a mental representation of the different sounds on the journey. There were frying sounds in the air condition. I heard opening, creaking and banging of doors. There was a port of some patient making crackling sounds when it was flushed. And, sounds of those machines every calling for help when fluid was low, or medication was completed.

I taxied into a room that had huge state-of-the-art machines waiting for me, to be used at the touch of a button. Obeying the request of the technician, I uncovered my upper body and lay supine on a not-so-soft cot-like bed neatly wrapped with several layers of sheets. She plastered gel to the head of a microphone-like instrument attached by a cord to a machine, and while I tried to relax, the technician rolled the head of the instrument clockwise and counterclockwise, over my abdomen and along the walls of my chest and took pictures. I felt the instrument sunk into my body every time she rolled it over me. I strained my eye to see what the monitor was showing, but I just couldn't make sense of it.

My darling wife sat beside me and waited patiently. She told me that the technician took fifty-four pictures. These, of course, confirmed and supported the data that the disease that sought to ravish my body was indeed leukemia.

The atmosphere in the lab was deathly cold. It made me wonder what physical death would be like. The procedure took about forty-five minutes. I was greatly relieved when this task was over. After that, I was transported back to my room incident free, treated to an invigorating cup of hot tea, instructed about what to expect the next day, and left to grapple with my thoughts and prepared to rest for the night.

Early the next morning, promptly at 4:00 a.m., the nurses came in haste. They shook me gently. "We need to take you to the lab as we promised last night." Being aware of the frigid atmosphere of the lab and being cognizant of the frailty of my immune system, I requested that they blanket me warmly. They quickly obeyed and wheeled me on my own limousine, my bed again, to the radiology lab. This time, to have a PICC line installed in my arm, under my left bicep, leading into my chest.

As I lay on my back, the technician administered anesthetic, and inserted the line, forty-seven millimeters long, looking more like an intravenous line but more sophisticated. It was tunneled through a large vein in my arm and guided into the main artery near my heart where blood flowed quickly. Then the technician sutured the PICC line in place and covered the site with a sterile bandage. An X-ray was done to make sure that the PICC line was in the right place. The entire procedure took approximately one and a half hours. I felt a little discomfort during this procedure but not to the point that I must even groan.

This line, in my case, was carefully and conveniently kept in place to facilitate the administering of chemotherapy drugs and other lifesaving fluids, as well as to draw blood for lab testing. This was a great relief to me, because the nurses didn't have to stick me every time for some weeks until my first round of chemo ended. They kept the line in place, for convenience. The line also relieved my fear of the needle. Probably not like other patients but when I saw the needle my veins become rigid

Also, besides the discomfort, I had to protect the line from pulling out, and I had to be especially careful when I bathed. I couldn't get it wet, because the wound was susceptible to infection. The least bit of moisture could cause me a whole lot of trouble. This was real scary, because the nurses told a few stories of people who jumped in pools or immersed themselves in their bathtubs while the line was still in their arms, and it had deadly consequences. Therefore, I usually covered the line and the wound with special plastic, and then bathe.

The Oncologist explained the procedure for my treatment. The first phase was called, the induction therapy, which normally would get me into remission. In this phase, I was induced with 7 + 3 plus Velcade chemotherapy but I didn't achieve remission on day 14 as was expected. Therefore, I was given five more days of cytarabine and two more days of daunorubicin. Finally, the Leukemia went into remission. To keep me safe during remission, consolidation maintenance therapy was given.

Remission is a temporary or permanent stage of the decrease that manifests it or shows no characteristics of a disease. In this phase, the patient has no threatening signs or symptoms.

I must give a word of caution to my reader, however, because this is where many patients fall prey. They assume that they are alright, whereas, the remission may be temporary. Chances are that the disease can return with devastating consequences if transplant or surgery doesn't take place shortly. If a complete remission is achieved and no further therapy is given, over 90 percent of patients will have a recurrence of the disease in weeks or months. It's for this reason that consolidation is given immediately after achieving remission. These treatments are given as closely together as possible. The more intensive the chemotherapy and the closer together the courses of therapy are given, the less chance the leukemia has of returning (CancerConnect.com, the leading online social network for patient care).

I lay on my back and gave keen attention to the oncologist. My chest rose and fell in rapid motion. I breathed deeply to relieve my anxiety. The oncologist took note and assured me that I shouldn't be afraid.

The oncologist provided me with literature so that I could satisfy my own curiosity and upgrade my knowledge. So, I started reading about Leukemia and did some research. One book I read was "*Understanding Leukemia,*" from the Leukemia & Lymphoma Society," which explained the details of the disease, enough to make me be somewhat conversant about the unknown causes, its progression, and its treatment. In passing though, I should explain that the leukemia that attacked me was the most acute, aggressive leukemia (AML). It needed to be treated as soon as possible after diagnosis. This my oncologist worked proactively to correct with the induction phase of my treatment. Following a time line, this was February 18, 2014. Two full weeks after admission.

4

FACED WITH MY OWN CHALLENGES and the confidence and prospect of total - healing, I embarked upon a quest to challenge the men, who came in contact me. I questioned then about their medical status. Thus, I would ask, "When last have you gone for a medical? I bet your doctor had wonderful things to say about your health."

Strangely, most responses they gave seemed to revolve around the same confession. "Oh, I did my blood works last week or the week before, and it was good."

"Good in what sense?" I'd inquire.

Some would beat around the bush, others responded frankly or sometimes jovially. They describe how healthy they were. They would emphasize and the exercise they did and the food they ate daily to support a healthy lifestyle. This was commendable indeed, I'd say. Yet I noticed that the conversations followed the same, or almost the same, pattern.

This pattern was strange but not surprising to me, in that I'd been following the instructions of a primary physician for more than six years. He joked one day and said, "Mr. Harding, dead men can't pay doctors." This was quite cordial. Yet, if this was taken out of context, and one should read into the statement, one could get some mileage in a discussion. Consequently, when one delved into an argument and began to ask the whys and what-ifs and how could he, this would seem quite reasonable to the naked eye. But Hey, that was the nature of the relationship between my primary physician and me. We could chitchat about anything and make jokes. This helped to establish the cordiality with which we were both comfortable. Yet this seemed to be a dangerous precedent on which to make such joke, when the enormity of the outcome was based on scientific data. We had a good laugh, but, probably, it could've been a moment too early to make what turned out to be such a snide remark.

Yet we rarely seemed to have a discussion outside the framework where we discussed blood pressure or he either commended or counseled me on the state of my prostate, cholesterol, or blood sugar health. This was solid advice, and I trusted his wise counsel.

However, eventually, I came to realize that all this information was only part of the issue. "Phlebotomy—the act or removing or drawing blood from the circulatory system through a cut, incision, or puncture to obtain blood samples for testing—carried a far more untapped importance in the function of the pathology." That is, the branch of medicine dealing with the essential nature of disease, especially changes in body tissues and organs.

Furthermore, as evidenced by scientific research, the most essential aspect of blood deals with blood count, specifically white blood cell and platelet count. Significantly, the white blood cell (White Blood Cell) count is used as part of a complete process to screen for different diseases. Most importantly, it can also be used to diagnose an infection or inflammatory process and to detect diseases, such a leukemia and immune system disorders. Likewise, white blood cells are used as a monitoring system. During my leukemia attack, the doctors watched my white blood cell counts very closely. It helped them to observe changes in the functions of the bone marrow. A (WBC) count is normally ordered also as part of the complete blood count (CBC), which may be performed when an individual undergoes a routine health examination. The test may be done when someone has general signs and symptoms of an infection such as fever, chills, body aches, pain, and headache.

Similarly, platelets are one of the most important aspects of the human blood. It plays a significant role in the clotting of blood. During an injury, it is the platelets that prevent excessive loss of blood. When the blood f lows, the platelets coagulate and become a plug to cover the blood vessel holes. When platelet counts are very low, they may make the patient very fatigued and restless. The skin becomes very thin and sensitive, which causes it to bruise very easily. A person can suffer from prolonged bleeding problems and have blood in the urine or stool, bleeding gums, and nosebleeds as well. This condition can also interfere with a person's healing process, especially after a surgery. Therefore, doctors, especially primary physicians, must monitor blood counts with painstaking care. This is where I think a primary physician can fall short, of verifying evidence. It takes a keen mind, lots of experience and a sense of devotion to one's work.

However, one can make a case to exonerate a doctor, if, in his opinion, he believes that his patient is healthy and shows no other symptoms by cogent evidence of blood sample. Yet observation, experience, and conjecture, though profound for making a diagnosis, are far from being perfect science. Therefore, it behooves one to solicit further evidence from other proven scientific methods to rule out symptoms of threatening disease. This is a rule of thumb, which is "a principle with broad application." It isn't intended to be strictly accurate or reliable for every situation. However, it's an easily learned and easily applied procedure for approximately calculating or reaching some value, or making some decision" (*Wikipedia, the Free Encyclopedia*). *Merriam-Webster* says it more bluntly: "A method or procedure based on experience or common sense."

Here's a perfect example. When I was diagnosed with acute Leukemia, the hematologist carried out his phlebotomy function, then requested further an in-depth study to confirm his diagnosis.

At first, he said, "Your blood shows some negatives," meaning that it was inconsistent with a healthy bone marrow. He promised to follow up when he got back to me in a few days.

Again, the case can be made that one may asking too much of the primary physician by expecting him or her to do specialized functions. Yet, once you assume the role of family physician, your role automatically becomes specialized. The big picture is that physicians should keep their patients in good health. That should evoke bold important questions that must be asked, because it takes but one further step to follow the trends in observing the blood sample.

Yet, herein lies the real-truth. Lab technicians only test and report on what the doctor orders, and this is strict medical procedure. However, there must, be some radical shift in the effort to save the lives of patients if one wants to prosper as a physician. No patient wants to go to a physician that has too many of them die often. While the onus is on the physician, the patient must take on some of the responsibility. Therefore, I've no intention of playing a blame game. A man of my age and stature should be more informed and alert. There's absolutely any excuse not to.

This brings in sharp focus the case of a lady in her middle forties whom I'll call Sandra. She saved her life by being proactive. She, ate healthy, walk two miles three times per week, stood five feet seven inches, and weighed one hundred fifty pounds. However, she developed a survival habit, which turned out to be not so good. She ate lots of peanut butter because it was filling and kept her satisfied longer in the days. As it turned out, it slightly spiked her cholesterol, but not to the point that it caused an adverse condition. She did several screening mammograms as part of her routine health procedure, which returned in negative results. Notwithstanding, she acted proactively in monitoring her health needs. After she examined her breasts, she discovered a small lump.

So, she decided to go to a different facility that had the services of 3-D imaging to do a mammogram with ultrasound screening.

It was confirmed that she had stage I cancer of the breast. The problem wasn't that screening wasn't done, but her former doctor trusted an MRI from a less-than-accurate imaging machine.

Consequently, Sandra wasn't aware of the workings of her body and how to perform breast examination, there would've been a later detection, which could've had catastrophic results. This scenario, though somewhat unrelated, can be applied to fully support the argument that doctors can't be too casual about a patient's health.

Blood works, has a profound effect for diagnosis when it is applied by doctors. Men and women must be informed about how low or how high their platelet, red blood cell, white blood cell, and hemoglobin counts are. This basic aspect of blood must be included in the report patients receive. Additionally, I believe, issues like high and low blood pressure, diabetes, and of course, all related maladies on an individual basis, must be taken into consideration. However, for those forty and above, even twice a year, primary physicians must provide report on the crux of the matter. These are the imperatives mentioned above! If carefully monitored, everyone can control blood sugar, high blood pressure, and cholesterol counts that are out of balance, with diet and proper exercise.

5

OVER THE YEARS, I HAVE developed a special way as to judge how healthy I was, based on my doctor's affirmation and my healthy eating habit and exercise. Undoubtedly, I built my confidence based on what he said: "If anything looks seriously wrong in your blood report, I would contact you. You don't have to worry." This was supposed to be the gospel truth, but it didn't materialize when it mattered. Once or twice, the nurse contacted me and cautioned me to beware of my borderline blood sugar and to watch my cholesterol. Hence, there was no adverse reaction or positive response to my blood report. As long, as my health remained this way, I was very healthy. Therefore, it seemed quite logical to think and assume that I had strong resistance against disease and infection. This was simply as I say, I ate right, and exercised to fit the bill, and had my physician's approval. But I was so wrong.

My brother was in a dissimilar situation, in that, unknowingly, we had the same physician but fortunately, he was one of those who inherited different gene traits from our bloodline. Therefore, he wasn't susceptible to this disease as I was. However, after I was diagnosed, I'd a conversation with him, only to find out that we both were being seen by the same physician. However, the very strangest things were taking place. He couldn't recall a single occasion when he went for the results of his blood works and had a totally different response than the one I was accustomed to getting.

Seemingly, there was indeed a similar pattern with the way this physician operated. He chitchatted during examination, and you were assured that you were just fine. My brother was, indeed. He was made aware of the state of his cholesterol, blood sugar, and prostate health, since he didn't have blood pressure or diabetes issues. Therefore, he was in perfectly good health. Clearly this was dissimilar to my case. When I told him of my experience, he was livid. He searched and found all his reports and examined them thoroughly. Fortunately, he had no need to panic. This evidence could suggest that physicians must treat patients on an individual basis. Consequently, if greater consideration is given to reporting on blood counts, it would make physicians' work much more thorough, scientific, and safer for all patients.

Quick questions, must be considered, "Was this the norm for other physicians? Was this the way they all operated? Or, just coincidentally, was it normal in my case, for me to assume that I was healthy, when half the truth hadn't been revealed? For I exuded confidence. I lived life to the fullest. I supported a healthy lifestyle. I followed research and latest trends, which made perfect sense. My diet was mainly fish and vegetables, baked potatoes, and fresh fruit juices. I took a multivitamin tablet, a vitamin D and sometimes small amounts of E, and 1,000 mg of vitamin C daily. I also took 1,000 mg of omega-D3 daily. I rarely wavered from this path. On Sundays, I ate brown stew chicken, fish, and occasionally a bit of oxtail, when my wife made us a Sunday treat. As a matter of fact, at my workplace, I conveniently volunteered to stop eating in the teachers' lunchroom because there was a clerk who worked in the office, who was allergic to fish. Therefore, when I was diagnosed with cancer it dropped like a bombshell on the staff, who tried in vain to get answers. "How could this be? He eats so healthy." Plus, I went to the gym three times per week and exercise. This was so true, because I had my accustomed workout the very night I received the terrible news. The unbelievable was true: I had cancer. I couldn't reverse it by my own effort. I could only reach out to the one who is my maker and friend. I'd neither signs nor symptoms, so this was indeed an unimaginable blow.

For years, I beguiled myself into believing that what you don't know won't hurt you, and I flippantly used this trite, colloquial, unsubstantiated statement to defend myself in conversations. I was a staunch proponent of spreading this blatant lie. To be honest, I was totally convinced that I was right. What I didn't know would never hurt me. Yet, this was one of those cases where ignorance wasn't bliss. I learned that truth in a wakeup call. What your doctor doesn't say will hurt you; what he does say could hurt you as well. It's like saying, "You are damned if you do and damned if you don't." To put the truth in perspective, some disease will strike even if one carries the doctor around in one's wallet or purse.

Let's look at a simple but far-from-being-unrealistic case. Assume that, there is a man with cancer and doesn't know that he has, a possible tumor in his lungs. The longer he lives in that state, the more it will take hold of his system. One day he collapses. Potentially, he loses consciousness and should have died. This could have been fatal were it not for the effective action of some proactive person who wasted little time and shouts, "Call 911, call, call!" They rush him to the emergency room. Oh boy, too late—but no, not yet! There was one who was gifted and well capable to do what was almost impossible for him. A year later, he was saying thanks for saving his life.

The truth is, it doesn't take rocket science to prove that if he'd known earlier, he might not have had to go through that trauma. Truth is, what this man didn't know could have cost him his life. Point taken!

One can safely assume that no one was monitoring his blood count, or he wasn't being attended to by a physician. The warning signs of his blood count went undetected or neglected. Likewise, serious intervention of a skilled hematologist wasn't sought.

In my case, I was just casually informed about my count, with no emphasis or sense of urgency that I ought to do something immediately. I didn't know the seriousness of this situation. I wasn't referred to a specific hematologist until my cell count was extremely low.

When I'd respond to the casual suggestion of my primary physician, I learned on February 17, 2014, the extent of my fate. This was indeed my wakeup call. After six years of entrusting my most precious commodity, my health, to a physician who should've had my best interest at heart, he casually told me on my last visit to him, "Mr. Harding, I notice that your platelets are getting lower."

"My what?" I asked. Pardon my ignorance. It was the first time I was hearing about what had become a hematological crisis that wasn't treated urgently. Unfortunately, I procrastinated unwittingly, in getting an early date with the hematologist, I delayed for probably two to three weeks, for reasons beyond my control. Of course, I had to depend on when the appointment was available.

"I want you to go and see a hematologist to understand what is happening in your blood," my primary physician said. *"And I want you to know that it's not anything I see that jumps out at me why I'm sending you. But your platelets are getting on the lower side, and I want you to get checked out. It is nothing to fear. I won't let you die."* Clearly, this was an understatement. This underscores the lack of urgency and the ineffective way information was disseminated. It was then that I kept the appointment with the hematologist. His report, supposedly, should've shocked me, but I refused to be surprised.

The hematologist was a man of almost equal proportions, seemed quite short behind the desk, probably about five feet six or seven inches tall. He was dressed in dark pants and a white shirt and tie. He spoke his request to a computer that responded to him. Subsequently, he sent me to do an MRI. When the results came back, all my blood counts were on the lower side. Hemoglobin, white blood cells, platelets, red blood cells, and every other count were lower than the average range. My white blood cell was 1.7, the average range being 3.5–10.0, and my platelets were 72, while the average range is 140–400. Yet my physician said it wasn't anything he saw that jumped out at him. Therefore, he sent me for a second opinion, and he added insult to injury: he wouldn't let me die. He had no clue as to the magnitude of the silent catastrophe bomb that was waiting to explode in my life.

I leave this to public scrutiny, for my readers to make a judgment. It was for this reason I said that this was a dangerous precedent on which to make such a serious joke, when the outcome was dependent on scientific imperative data. That was why the premise on which the joke was made left many unanswered questions. Does he have the experience? I think so. Could've done better? Dear me, I think he could've. If so, why did he use such trite remarks and made such casual jokes? I believe that in the spirit of the moment he was joking. So, how could I place all the blame on him? A man of my age and stature ought to be more informed. Therefore, should I lay the blame squarely on him? I shouldn't think so I should've been more attentive.

However, this was only the tip of the iceberg. I went to death's door. Yes, I've beaten the odds. My divine mentor didn't allow me to die because of neglect or procrastination. He made me a promise, and He honors his word above his name. His timing was extraordinarily perfect. Therefore, this message will but inspire men and women to be more attentive to their health needs. When they go to the doctor, they must engage their physician in a discussion about how to unpack their lab report. Men, especially, you are supposed to lead in the home and be the breadwinners. You need to be more aware of your rights and the right questions to ask. Men, who are supposed to be the trendsetters for future generation, ought to be more responsible. Unless you ask relevant question, doctors assume that you understand. It isn't enough to shake hands after your examination, write a check, and say good-bye. There must be, a more engaging process.

After leaving the physician's office, the process must continue. Today, thanks to computers and search engines, there's no excuse. Those who are interested can find almost any subject or topic on the web they wish to read. For the first time, the "Pew Research Center's Internet & American Life Project has found that cell phone ownership among adults has exceeded 90%. Cell phones are now being used by 91% of adults, according to the survey conducted between April 17 and May 19, of 2,252 adults." Therefore, one should take the report and research each topic to see what it means. One can't just collect a copy of the report and stuff it in a drawer somewhere. There must be some sensibility on the part of patients. It isn't enough just to go with what your physician says.

6

AFTER SPENDING SEVEN MONTHS in Palm Hospital, from February to July 2014, a series of unfavorable developments affected my relationship with the hospital. During late July, I became very agitated. I was prompted to seek further opinion about my health. To say I was uneasy, would speak it mildly. I was very restless. I was fatigued. I couldn't sleep at nights. I got sleep aid tablets, but I hate to ingest them, so I put them away and didn't complain about sleeping. The opinion I tried to seek, wasn't purely my decision, but the advice of my donor's wife. I reacted because I got to understand that my name wasn't on the schedule for bone marrow transplant during the summer. At that time, the Leukemia was in remission. Hence, I couldn't understand what was preventing the procedure. I believe that I was waiting longer than I should. The problem, I saw was that there could be a reversal, and I didn't want to go back on chemotherapy.

A second thing that made me uneasy was, financial misunderstandings. I was unprepared for the bills that were coming to me daily. Instead of getting stressed, I should've forwarded them to my Insurance Company. Yet I didn't do that or speak to somebody who was knowledgeable. So, I would go about with this weight on my chest. When I lay on my back it was as if this weight was pressing me through the matrass.

Then thirdly, was my own view of the whole affair. My vision was very clouded. I looked no further than the four walls of Palm Hospital for answers. I was very impressed with the work there, and I found myself vacillating between opinions. By August, I should've received the bone marrow transplant and on my way to recovery. Yet, there wasn't even the mention of a date when the procedure would take place. Consequently, with all this uncertainty, I found it difficult to break the emotional ties from those whom I admired so much and who'd made an indelible imprint on my life. One thing I knew, was that everything wasn't going exactly the way I wanted them to go in terms of my treatment. Therefore, there was the restlessness in my spirit.

The summative response to these circumstances that I grappled over, could never come at a better time. It was addressed by the phone call from my sister-in-law. Then, a quotation I remembered from the biblical text: (KJV) "*14Where no counsel is, the people fall: but in the multitude of counsellors there is safety.*" My safety was in counsel from my sister-in-law who was not from the medical field.

Henceforth, I broke the shackles of indecision. "I sought for another opinion. I just asked the department of oncology to fax my records to the hospital that I chose. Then my new primary physician told me about two hospitals which coordinated with Palm Hospital. First, he told me about Fair View in Southern Miami that did regular stem cell transplant and then River Buff in the northern part of the state that did substantially more. In comparison, Palm Hospital didn't have a record of such magnitude. In fact, Palm Hospital was just in the beginning phases of stem cell transplant.

One of my drawbacks was that I'd a good insurance policy but just didn't know how to make it work for me. "*Indeed, the heart of the prudent gets knowledge; for the ear of the wise seeks for it*" (Proverbs 18:15 KJV). Now that I was gaining knowledge, I had to seek the wisdom of apply it. So, in this light, I found the truth and fortified myself with expert information. In addition, I gained this insight also from the case manager assigned to me by my insurance company. He was informative, knowledgeable, and candid in his remittance of information. Not that he set out to convince me, but with the sheer weight of his experience, I was persuaded to act fast on it by faith.

Palm Hospital was out of network for bone marrow transplant with my insurance company. I was now certain. That was a shock, because I really wanted to complete everything there. It meant that if I remained there, I'd be treading on dangerous ground. Having been associated with the hospital from February until as late as August I believed that registration in the bone marrow transplant program was automatic. This wasn't so. There had to be this conference over your case, where it is deliberated over before your selection and that meeting never seemed to be planned.

There seemed to have been some misunderstanding between my insurance company and Palm Hospital also. For whatever reason, I remained a medical patient, wasn't clear to me. According to my Case Manager; a medical patient is different from one who is registered as a transplant patient. Accordingly, Palm Hospital wasn't part of the insurance company's Life source network. Obviously, this was a big disappointment to me. He further explained that if I remained there at Palm Hospital for the transplant, it would probably cost me an enormous sum of money even if the insurance paid a portion of the cost. Though Medicare would get involved; it would still be very costly whereas, if I went to Fair View or River Buff, it would cost me a fraction of the cost or nothing at all out of pocket. This was my salvation. Based upon his recommendation, or rather his suggestion, I decided to go to Fair View Comprehensive Cancer Center for consultation, I did get through and it cost me nothing out of pocket.

Although my presumptive leaving caused a conflict in my mind, with reluctance, I made the appointment. This meant wrenching me from the people to whom I'd become so attached. I'd miss the very good relationship and treatment from the nurses, plus the convenience to get to and from the hospital, that my wife had become used to. I was torn between two opinions, whether to leave or to stay.

However, other developments forced my hand. It so happened that I began receiving several bills, sometimes three every other day. I mean $600, 700, and even thousands of dollars yet I had insurance. I reported this astronomical and almost daily occurrence to my case manager. who reiterated and confirmed the point he made about the different treatment offered to a medical patient as opposed to a transplant patient.

Part of the chaotic situation made worse, was that I didn't only get these bills, but to rub salt in my emotional wounds, I began getting letters from collection agencies. For instance, I'd to send in documentary evidence to show proof of payment of a $1000 bill. Of course, this wasn't the only problem. It wasn't that I didn't want to pay my bill. For safety, I'd to check with the insurance company to see if the claims were warranted. Fortunately, many of them I didn't have to paid.

It cost me far more out of my pocket at Palm Hospital for the first seven months before the transplant than I paid at Fair Vi pre- and post-transplant over one- and a half year period. This was all because I didn't understand the difference in both hospital admission programs. The real problem, though, wasn't only the bills and letters but also that I couldn't get in touch with the agencies. They kept me on hold, thanked me for calling, and said they would be right back. Sometimes I waited long periods, twenty minutes sometimes, then they hung up on me. This was frustrating.

I also had another conflict with my insurance. Palm Hospital wanted me to join Medicare Part B to absorb some of the costs. This was a very attractive offer. However, I would've to retire from my job before they'd honor my request. This means that I'd have lost all the benefits from my insurance, being retired. Upon retirement. the social worker told me that Medicare would be the number one

1 insurance, and my insurance company Cigna would become the alternate. When a bill was sent to me, I'd forward it to Medicare, which would honor a portion, and then my insurance company would pay the rest. It was because of all the afore mentioned developments, that I made the appointment to see an oncologist at Fair View. However, before I speak of all the happenings at Fair View, I must tell the story of the ominous misdeeds that threatened my very life.

While I was in Palm Hospital, I completed a few rounds of chemotherapy, that obviously sapped my energy. I was very weak. The nurse posted a sign on the chart in my room, "Fall Alert." I wasn't supposed to leave my room without the escort of someone, the same for going to the restroom as well as taking a shower.

However, one night, nature overpowered me. I'd to pass my urine urgently because of the extra liquid that was being pumped into my body, to f lush out the chemo. With this urge, I jumped up and failed to find one of the urine cups at my bedside. The nurse aide who made my bed had taken them to the restroom after cleaning and didn't return them to the usual spot in my room. I spun over to the bedside table where they were kept, but they weren't there. I looked beside the bed.

Yet, they were nowhere in sight. I panicked in the dim light. In the meantime, my faucet let loose, and streams of contaminated saline began to wet my pajama. It was not capable of stopping the flow.

I rushed to get to the restroom while urine flushed the floor. On reaching for the door, I missed it in the dim light and went sprawling backward with an un-controlled crash. Luckily, I believe, the Holy Spirit cushioned my fall when my head hit something like a Styrofoam box. I heard the deafening pop. I was more frightened than hurt. I went slipping, sliding, and bumping here and there on the slick floor. This was the only time that I failed to admire the beautiful floor. As quickly as I could, I gathered my disheveled self from the f loor, and looked for the box that saved my life. I turned on the bright light, but there was no sign of a box. Then I concluded that the crack I heard must have been absorbed by my supernatural "big brother." He must have taken the impact. Just like on the cross he was wounded for my transgression, He was bruised for my sins. Like the song says I should have been crucified, I should've suffered and died, I should have hung on the cross in disgrace, but Jesus God Son to my place." "He was there just in time to rescue me rescue me." The Promise Keeper, Miracle and Way Maker was, there all the time. What the devil meant for evil the Lord turned it around for good. "The LORD your God is with you, the Mighty Warrior who saves. (Zephaniah 3:17) He will take great delight in you; in his love he will no longer rebuke you but will rejoice over you with singing." "Psalm (46 :1) God is my refuge and strength, a very present help in trouble.

Therefore, will not we fear, though the earth be removed, and though the mountains be carried into the midst of the sea; nor the waters thereof roar and be troubled." (Psalm 46:2). I started shaking but with fading strength, I consciously cleaned myself, changed my pajamas, and timidly, step by step, made my way from the wet floor to the bed, which luckily didn't get any of the downpour.

Then I realized the seriousness of what could've happened. I shivered greatly. With trembling hand, I rang the emergency alarm and reported my fall. With urgency, several nurses and the doctor on duty rushed into my room, asking questions. "Where did you hurt?" "Why didn't you call?" "Raise your hands. Open your eyes." The doctor shone a light in my eyes. "Do you feel any pain?" To all these questions, I replied in the negative. "Keep an eye on him. We want to be sure he is fine."

Yet, I was far from okay. About two weeks after the event, I began feeling excruciating pain on the left side of my face, radiating to my left eye. The doctors carried out MRIs and CAT scans and physically examined my head but couldn't find what was causing the pain, but no one referred to the fall. One thing I didn't disclosed was that members of my family had suffered aneurisms in the past.

One sister had five and became a vegetable. Her son had one and he died. The doctors prescribed various powerful pain relievers, but none worked for more than a few minutes. I would try to sleep, and if I did it was only for a few minutes, then the pain would return just as before, within the time before another dose could be administered. So, if it returned two or three hours before, I would groan and cry until the next dose was administered. Sometimes a nurse would rub my head and tried to offer some comfort. Yet, they had other duties, they could give so much time and no more. Then when the next dose was administered I would be so worked up, it didn't work as well.

At the start of the pain, a senior oncology specialist, Dr. Gordon, went on leave. Two weeks later, he returned and paid a visit to my room and remarked, "It's too long for a man to be in pain." He prescribed a strong dose of morphine, and a nurse administered the drug in tablet form. For the first time in two weeks, I'd a good night of uninterrupted sleep. He also recommended a warm pad on which to rest my head. This brought me some measure of relief. However, can anyone imagine my disappointment? Nowhere on my bead seemed comfortable to place my head. After trying to fit my head on the pillow in several ways, I got up and pace the floor and groaned. Sometimes I felt that I would have lost my balance, so I returned to my bed of misery. Yet Doctor Gordon denied giving me another dose of the good stuff. "It is not the cure Mr. Harding it was only temporary relief to get you some sleep. Did you sleep well? Good we will continue to search for the solution to that problem." I was discharged from the confines of Palm Hospital to sleep in my bed for two nights after I'd been away for nearly three months.

It was a joy and full of glory to be home. Nothing was impossible. I dwell in the realm of exciting possibilities. The way in the tunnel was a bright as day. I slept like a baby. The calmness I felt was the prelude to the thunder-clap which was awaiting me. I got up early and looked around my kitchen and tried to see if there was anything that I could challenge my appetite. My darling wife, came to my rescue. She always seems to know what to offer. She served me hot Milo beverage with rich creamer and nutmeg. Suddenly, she looked at me and said, "Honey, your left eye is drooping."

I went to the mirror to confirm it. The lid of my left eye was halfway closed. However, since I was going to the hospital for a checkup, I didn't pay it much attention.

By the time I got there, it got worse, but the Ontime, omnipresent Light in the Darkness got there before me and delayed my Oncologist in the hall way, at Pines Hospital.

When he saw me, he said with a sense of urgency in his voice, "Your eye is drooping Mr. Harding. This doesn't look good. Doesn't look good one bit."

Immediately he ordered an emergency MRI and had me chauffeur driven in my usual limousine to the radiology lab down the hallway. As he had said, it didn't look good. I was diagnosed with a massive aneurism at the back of my head, just above my neck on the left side. Time sped up so fast that I lost track of what happened next. Whether it was anesthetic, or I lost consciousness, it was not clear to me. However, as it turned out, I was transported to Fair Prospect Hospital and had surgery done immediately.

The scripture says: "And it shall come to pass that before they call He will answer and while they are yet speaking He will hear". "Isaiah: 24) This was the hand of my divine deliverer that protected me in that fall.

His sovereign guidance directed the Oncologist to spot the signs and take proactive action. I was placed in ICU for recovery. This was a time of extreme suffering, which reminded me of this word: *"Blessed be God, even the Father of our Lord Jesus Christ, the Father of mercies, and the God of all comfort; Who comfort us in all our tribulation, that we may be able to comfort them which are in any trouble, by the comfort wherewith we ourselves are comforted of God." (Corinthian 1:2-4)*

I was delirious, confused, and embarrassed. I was ridiculed and disrespected. But who am I to speak about mockery? "The chief priests and scribes stood there, vehemently accusing Jesus. And even Herod and his soldiers ridiculed and mocked Him." (St Luke 23:11-12)

One night, in my delusion, I was to be transported to the radiology lab for a procedure. I asked the male nurse assigned to me to allow me to make a telephone call to my wife, because my cellphone was uncharged. He denied me access to the call. I knew this to be ordinary routine. You don't need administrative clearance to make a telephone call. If my Oncologist, the surgeon or the hospital knew of this incident it would not have been allowed. When I asked him why, he rudely retorted, "Because I say so." Things became confusing. Why did he refuse?" I asked myself. In my confused state, I saw him produced a red syringe and placed it in the upper left-side pocket of his uniform shirt. I was confused but not blind. I became very suspicious and afraid of him. I told him straight up to leave my room. He carried the syringe with him, so it seemed, to the lab but invited another male to come and accompany us. He didn't inject me.

When I reached the lab, I asked the technician not to allow him in the room. Accordingly, the second person accompanied me inside. To be truthful, I can't remember the details about the procedure or what went on but what I believed I saw was scary.

When I returned to my room, the second nurse administered an injection to me. Surprisingly, 'twas a similar red syringe that he used. When he put out the instruments on the table, the male nurse threw the syringe from his pocket on the table as well. In surprise inquired of him why he threw the syringe on the table, and he said, "To be discarded." I said to him, "Is that the way you discard used syringes?" He didn't reply. This caused me to wonder. Did I see right. Probably not. I had double vision. But nothing was wrong with my hearing. I heard him clearly, he said the syringe was to be discarded.

Foolishly, I shared my concern with a native who spoke my dialect. It turned out that she joined forces with the male nurse who jokingly, "Stab-me-in-the-back." She made humor at my expense. They made fun of my speech and thought that I was crazy old man. They showed no sympathy nor concern for my suffering. Not that I'm blaming them for their ignorance, and lack of insight. Not that they were to pamper me as was treated at the former hospital. Yet for the dignity and professional behavior that employees should demonstrate, the one they pledge to uphold in their training, they should be more responsible. Even if they talk softer that I the patient couldn't hear them but, no, they were on speakerphone.

This wasn't the only embarrassing problem I suffered. I was constipated for over five days. I suffered greatly. "Because of the voice of the enemy, Because of the pressure of the wicked; For they bring down trouble upon me And, in anger they bear a grudge against me. My heart is in anguish within me, And the terrors of death have fallen upon me. Fear and trembling come upon me, and horror has overwhelmed me…anguish within me; the terrors of death have fallen on me. Fear and trembling have beset me; horror has overwhelmed me." (Psalm 54: 4-5) I groaned loudly. I groan softly. It seemed so embarrassing, I didn't tell anyone. Since I was unofficially diagnosed to be crazy, no one looked in at me. On the fifth night, I revealed my discomfort to an attending nurse who had just changed shift for the night. I was so glad to see someone who could talk to me. She turned and spoke to a nurse aide from one of the islands of the Caribbean. I recognized the distinct accent. She talked like me. She told her, "This patient needs a suppository."

That very rude, disrespectful young woman laughed and laughed at me until she cried. Then she rubbed salt in my wound when turned to me, still laughing and said, "Whe you need suppository fa, man?" And, she continued her embarrassing, humiliating laughter.

I restrained myself, really restrained my tongue. I was too shocked and in pain to reply. She didn't help as she was supposed to do.

While I lingered in pain and disbelief, I fell into a brief doze. I woke with the urge to go to the bathroom. I scrambled from my bed. I staggered to the door. I reached the haven of my quest and sat in anticipation. To my relief, after some straining, burning and pushing, I had the most beautiful release. I cleaned myself, but there was no sign of the destructive release on the wipe. It was as dried and hard as wood. I went to bed, but I left the monster standing upright in the toilet bowl, as straight as a light pole. For diagnostic purpose, I was asked not to f lush when I used the bathroom. Therefore, it told its own tale of victory to the Aide who had to f lush it several times to release it.

At this place, I silently went through Hades. I had an argument with one of the island nurses who wanted to bathe me. I refused her offer and insisted that when my wife came, she'd do it. This didn't go well with her and her colleagues. They felt that I was a difficult, uncooperative patient.

This seemed to take its toll on relationships one night thereafter. My friend and brother in the Lord Patrick Folks brought me some chicken to challenge my appetite. I found it appetizing. Can you imagine the broad smile I wore on my face. I dove in and was enjoying it. My friend, was so pleased, he just sat and looked at me. I scooped up some from the dish and raised the spoon to my mouth, and I looked up again and saw this island nurse staring at me with her hand on hip and her elbow bent upward, akimbo. She was militant in her disposition. Her response was "I need to draw your blood." She didn't say now, but I seem to get her message. I shifted uneasily. I was embarrassed for my friend to witness this kind of treatment.

My friend looked at me, and I looked at him. "So, abrupt," he said. Then I responded, "Do you wish for me to finish eating, or you want me to do it right now?"

She wheeled away and didn't answer. I heard her talking in her speech, but I couldn't decipher it. I just didn't speak the language. I couldn't determine whether what she said was good or bad, but when she returned with her brazen and demanding attitude, her intentions were clear. She meant now.

I said to my friend, "I'm the Christian." I put away my food and offered her my hand. Unfortunately, I couldn't relax. Her effort didn't succeed in achieving what she intended. At least she was privileged embarrass herself. I grimace and cried and laugh. That added to her embarrassment and made me very uncomfortable. She couldn't find the vein after sticking me three times. In frustration, she called a colleague to perform the task. Yet in hindsight, this was part of the platform the Lord gave me. Granted that part of the time I was not in my right mind, but at times I was very conscious to put these issues in perspective, but I failed to grapple with the nature of these situation. I could've been more gracious. It would've made a difference.

However, with every dark cloud, there is a silver lining.

As I lay on my back in the dim light, half asleep one night after the last disrespectful treatment, two people, a man and a woman, suddenly invaded my presence, when they appeared at my bedside. My heart skipped a beat. Their faces were cloudy, but the form of their being was quite clear to me.

As a result, of the cloudy appearance of their faces, I couldn't judge their ages. The man was shorter than the woman, who was about five feet six inches tall and weighed about 180 pounds. He was dressed formally. He wore a beige brown suit, a white shirt, and a tie that matched his jacket. The lady weighed approximately 136 pounds. They were both of fair complexion, and they held hands.

The gentleman addressed his concern to me. "So, what is this I heard happening to you, man?" This sounded like the kind of address I would have heard from my island friends, 'Man.'

I began to tell him my woes, but as soon as I began to speak, I sort of turned my eye away and they vanished. I never saw them again. I thought it very strange. I wondered if I was dreaming. I never heard anything about them, nor did I make a report about this incident or any of the mistreatment. So, although these two could have been real, who could I report that as a believable story. They might seem unbelievable, since there was no record of them. I was more anxious to get out of that frustration than to make reports.

Yet, within a day later, I experienced my silver lining. I was visited by a physiotherapist who was assigned to my case. He worked with children to rehabilitate them after surgery. I was his adult Guinea pig. He was a tall, thin gentleman who spoke softly. He always dressed in a green hospital suit and soft-sole shoes. His name I don't remember, but he pushed me through some effective exercise that made me stronger. I could walk up two f lights of steps and walk on a straight line, though I stumbled. I could also stand on one leg with my hands outstretched sideways. So, he lavished praise for my effort. I could to raise my legs backward and forward, as he instructed. As a result, when a nurse came to evaluate my progress, she said my effort surpassed her expectation. I was released from the confines of Fair Prospect with recommendation for a physiotherapist and a field nurse to come to my house to work with me.

When I got out of the hospital, everything looked strange. I seem to be travelling in a different space and time. Everything seemed to be upside down or moving in two forms. This concerned me very much. I wonder if I was losing my sight. I further learned that it was double vision (diplopia).

"Double vision is the perception of two images of a single object seen adjacent to each other (horizontally, vertically, or obliquely) or overlapping. Diplopia is the medical term for double vision. Polyopia is the perception of three or more images of a single object overlapping each other.

Double vision is called "monocular" when the double image is perceived by an eye that is tested alone. In "binocular" double vision, each eye sees a single image when tested alone, but a double image is present when both eyes are opened.

There are dozens of causes of double vision, ranging from benign to life-threatening. Therefore, it is important for the doctor to carefully review the history and perform an examination to determine the cause and initiate appropriate treatment when necessary. Sometimes, emergency treatment is needed.

Most causes of monocular diplopia stem from poor focusing of light by the eye. Refractive errors (myopia, hyperopia, astigmatism) are causes. Dry eye (from a variety of causes such as meibomitis, Sjögren's syndrome, and decreased tear production following refractive surgery) can produce diplopia that varies with blinking. Cataracts (clouding of the natural lens) and posterior capsule opacification (which can occur after cataract surgery) are common in people over 60 years of age." While there are dozens of home treatments, I didn't have to apply any.

I went to see my optician, but he couldn't tell me anything about my condition. He was oblivious as to what was going on in my eyes. He recommended that I see another specialist, but I didn't follow up. Instead, I made an appointment to see a specialist at the Eye Institute at Fair View. So, not only did everything look strange, but when I walked, I lost my balance. I'd to walk with a walker to support myself from falling. However, before I got to the Eye Institute, the double vision disappeared.

In keeping with the instructions from the Fair Prospect, Jerome P. T. the physiotherapist, called me and made arrangement to come and work with me. When he came, I had to declare my consent to the treatment by signing a form. I was a bit skeptical about Jerome but that it didn't take long to change my opinion. He was an amiable guy but was businesslike. He was Hispanic, fair, about six feet tall, with broad shoulders, and weighed approximately 160 pounds. He'd a low haircut, and he was dressed semi-formally, in shirt and tie. I cooperated with Jerome like I did with the physiotherapist at the hospital. Likewise, he led me through different exercises.

The first thing that he did in his routine was to take my blood pressure, and midway between exercises, he repeated the process. Then, he attached two three-pound weights on my ankles and asked me to raise my legs slowly, and I repeated the exercise. I usually did three sets of tens. Then, he had me carry out other exercises that involved walking in a straight line, squatting, and raising my legs sideways, backward, and forward, to name a few of the paces he took me through. After seven lessons, he said good-bye and left me to work by myself, following the examples he gave.

I improved rapidly. I started doing leg raise, three sets of tens, while increasing the tempo. I improved to be able to raise my legs seventy-two times, doing six sets of twelve, while I sat on a couch. I also followed the other exercises that he taught me. So, I became stronger.

The other health person was Terry, who came to manage my case. She monitored my vital signs. She was Haitian, and she spoke broken English. She was about thirty-plus years old and was medium build. She weighed approximately 130 pounds. She wore thick lens glasses and had to keep the paper close to her eyes, to read. It took her forever to write her notes. I discontinued her service because I could take my vital signs and record them quite easily.

However, I needed time to recuperate after the great ordeal with the aneurysm. My oncologist recommended blood thinners, aspirin and Percocet tablets. These medications were safeguards against blood clotting. They weren't only blood thinners, but they also served as anti- platelet inhibitors. Therefore, often I went to the clinic for blood work at the pathology lab, I found that my counts were very low, like 11,000 or 15,000/μL. Because of this, I was given platelet transfusion very often. My platelet would raise to 26,000 or 36,000/μL, but in the next visit, it would tumble to 10,000/μL. This was quite a distraction. I'd be focused upon the notion that I was to and should do things to grow my platelets and white blood cell counts. Yet, this was unprofitable. This should have been after the transplant. I was recommended to engage in a cream cheese and f lag seed oil diet. This make me feel nauseous from upset stomach. I'd also mash two papaya leaves and try to drink it the juice, but this was so distasteful that I discontinued this approach. Similarly, I was recommended to drink moringa but that was also bad tasting.

These extra helpings that I ingested caused me to feel worse for hours. At the same time, my blood counts didn't change for the better. I was totally frustrated. My appetite was not good. The average weight for a five feet 6.5 height male is 154 pounds but I was weighing 129. I was like skin and bone. I was asked to remain at home for five weeks but take visits to Palm Hospital to check on my counts.

After the lapse of five weeks, I was back in Palm H the hospital for another round of chemotherapy. I had two high doses of cytarabine consolidation followed by Vedas. These medications were most distressing. I lost my hair again, developed purple-to-black nails, and suffered with mouth sores and anorexia. It was difficult for me to eat. I got hooked on soup for a while. I would drink soup four times per day, but I found it difficult to gain weight. Plus, I was fatigued in the afternoons. I was very restless. My feet were most uncomfortable. I tried to massage them, and I applied warm and ice pack, but things just seemed to remain the same. Now I learned to drink honey in hot water, warm milk or to take a hot bath.

I should've consulted the specialist, who performed the surgery two weeks after the procedure, but I never did because of all the seemingly endless medical issues above. My condition caused me to undergo test after test. These were some of the biggest distractions that kept me from getting help sooner.

7

NOW WE RETURNED TO THE Fair View saga. The date
was September 26. It was one of the best moves I made. It
promised much, and I approached it with great expectation. After
having blood drawing in the pathology lab, I had consultation with
the Oncologist. He found me a worthy candidate for a transplant.
He told me that the bone marrow stem cell transplant was critical
for my total recovery, though I was in remission.

By October 17, all arrangements and paperwork were put in
motion. The date was set for my admission to get the stem cell
transplant. In this light, several tests and procedures that were done
all came back with negative results. Results confirmed that I was
an ideal candidate, and this confirmed the Oncologist's findings of
eligibility for the transplant. So, the first hurdle was accomplished.
Therefore, November 4 was set for my date with destiny.

The total healing process would include chemotherapy. However,
before I'd get the stem cell transplant, I'd to undergo a conditioning
process of preparation. Also, I would need to find a donor right
away. This process had been an interesting one.

While I was at Palm Hospital, the bone marrow specialist
coordinator solicited my siblings to participate in a donor search
matchup. Packages were sent out to four available and able-bodied

men and women: Norma and Tyrone living in Canada, Joan living in Jamaica, and Neville living in Georgia, USA. Their task was to use a given suave, wipe it in the four quadrants of their mouth, package it, and return it. The packages were then sent to Lab Corp for analysis of each sample.

Weeks passed, and I anxiously awaited the report. With bated breath, I questioned each day if the results had arrived. Doctor Delgado and the coordinator of the Bone Transplant Unit Mrs. Sidney Ramus, came to my room. The physician said Mr. Harding we bring you good news. Immediately I removed the sheet from off my face and sat up. They both greeted me with pleasant smiles. I wasn't disappointed. The results came back as was anticipated. My most amiable brother of seventy-two years old achieved the highest prize. He returned a perfect match—10/10 matchup. This was remarkable. It was the ideal situation, but his age was questionable. Research showed that the best donors were those within the eighteen-to-sixty age bracket.

To compound the delicate problem of age, a real psychological battle began to wreak havoc on our lives. At first, my brother was very excited to be privileged to be my donor. I received the news with open arms and great expectation. I was elated beyond measure, but then, the uncertainty was the other side of the coin. I must confess that this was part of a long series of distractions.

They were clearly geared at contradicting everything that supported the truth about my healing. These began in the form of patterns personal attacks but mushroomed into bigger and bigger invasions. To this end, I don't think any patient was transported to the radiology lab as often as I was. I believe that I went to that lab more than twelve times per month for one thing or another. When it was not a pain in my arm, because of the fear of a blood clot; or it was a pain in my neck, causing fear of some neurological problem, you bet, I earned another ride on my limousine. Then. my abdomen started to cramp, which showed signs of intestinal infection. Each of these symptoms masked my recovery and necessitated my going to the radiology lab for a procedure, be it MRI, CAT scan or Ultrasound, also sending the stool or urine for testing. This was part of the stuff that made my Promise Keeper special. He comforted me in my sorrow, He soothe my pain when I was hurting. His word says: "Cast all your cares upon Him because He cares for you." 1st (Peter 5:7)

Then, there was a heart problem. This was amazing. It was a real drama. You know that moment, when the evil power tries to scare you. You are going to die moment, when. you cannot breathe. That was what I faced one day. I went for my regular oncology follow up. This was sometimes three days per week depending on the stability of my blood counts. I had a symptom which I thought was a heart attack. When I exhaled, I could not breathe in, so my breathing was shallow. I sat in the waiting room for more than half an hour struggling with this invasion. When I was called in I reported the condition. The nurse said asked me: "Why didn't you tell us before? You could've hurt yourself." The next split second, the fire rescue was sounding the alarm.

The rescuers came charging in, took me to their truck, check me out, put a tablet under my tongue, then rushed me to the emergency room. That cost me twenty-three hours of valuable time in the hospital to maintain regular standard procedure. However, like this seeming heart problem test, via an EKG, all other tests, returned negative results. It reached the point that when I felt discomfort, I didn't report them. I learned how to survive. These small opposing encounters came to make me strong. *Like Andrew Crouch said Through it all he learned to trust in Jesus, he learned to trust in God. If he never had a problem, I wouldn't know that God could solve them.* They were caused by the chemotherapy. As a result, I decided that whenever one of these symptoms rear its ugly head, it was temporary, and it would soon pass. Therefore, together, pain and discomfort were my close companions. But the blessings of the Lord made me rich and added no sorrow. Proverbs 19:22

Hence, from that point on, I strove to be positive. I tried not to entertain negative thoughts or giving them as answers. When I was asked: "How're you today?" I used one of the catch phrases, "Great" or "I'm just fine," and I said that with an attitude. They thought of me as great patient. All the nurses and physicians knew me as an exemplary patient. One day a Doctor remarked Mr. Harding you will get better soon.:." When they did their check up and left my room, I had to cover my head under the sheet sometimes and cried as I rested in the arms of Jesus, as the song says: "Safe in the arms of Jesus, Safe on his gentle breast, There, by his love overshared us, sweetly my soul shall be." I realized that I'd to speak things as I wanted them to be.

For these reasons, I should've kept that appointment, two weeks after the Aneurysm surgery done by Dr. Hibbert Wong. However, all these seemingly health maladies curtailed my time. I was delayed from seeing him until August 15. Surprisingly, this was my birthday. He gave me one of the best presents when he declared that the carotid artery in my neck that was severed and caused the aneurysm was healed. After he performed his examination, he said, "You don't need to take any more blood thinners, no aspirin, no Percocet." My heart danced with the singing of his words. I left his office very joyful. Yet Proverbs7:12 says danger lurks in the street. On my way, my driver and I, were, almost ran over by a large service truck at the intersection of Eight 26 and Miami Garden's Drive during torrential rain that made visibility poor.

Some of the distractions were impersonal, but they threatened to destabilize my confidence, none the-less. Of all the issues my brother had to deal with, he went through a period of the greatest psychological battles. He'd a longstanding pain in his navel, which threatened to take his life. He had pains night and day for which he couldn't find any solution. He was seen by many doctors, who seemed clueless to determine a reasonable diagnosis for his problem.

Consequently, in frustration, I asked that he be dropped from the donors list, and I told him. Surprisingly, in a few days, he was fine, but with him off the list, I didn't have a donor. One doctor diagnosed that he had irritable bowel syndrome; unknowingly, this left me without the key for my transplant, but not without hope.

My hope was ultimately in my Maker's hands. Regardless of what I faced, I would rally back to His Word. He who has started a good work in me will complete to the end. Therefore, I went through a period of drought myself when nothing seemed to be happening. I remember I went to a church service, during which a prophet prophesied with convincing accuracy, so it seemed. He called out people around me but didn't mention me. Like Job I questioned God. I wanted to know how a critically sick man who was recovering, would be overlooked by a prophet. If God was speaking to him then he should get a word for me. So, I challenged him after the service about my case. I confessed that I believed that I was healed and was not in remission. This would be a direct con-tradiction. I also told him about my donor. He told me not to worry about the donor, because the person on whom I was depending., might not be the one our Father had in mind. Therefore, I relaxed and waited for His move.

However, moments like these were very nerve-racking. Although I had trifles of uncertainty, I was convinced that my Redeemer intervened and healed me of this sickness. Furthermore, there were several incidents above that persuaded me to take this stand. As a matter of fact, the very person that prophet told me not to worry about became my donor, a perfect 10/10 match. I wasn't put off by what he said. I did not oppose him. I just kept it in my heart and believed in Jehovah Raphe. I cherished his words of truth, and in my moments of doubt and stress, I ministered to myself by rehearsing his promises, sometimes aloud and at other times silently. Sometimes I groaned pains of agony. A distress rocked my boat and threatened to capsize me in perilous waters. This reminded me of a song to the effect that a man saw, danger at sea

But: The good Captain commanded a boat to be lowered,

And with tender compassion He took me on board
And I'm happy today, all my sins washed away
In the blood of my Savior, and now I can say: Bless the
Lord; Bless the Lord.
From my Soul, I can say: Bless the Lord.

This was indeed time to bless the Lord. Therefore, when these psychological wars began to affect my brother, I was compelled to dismiss them as distractions. Yet, they were not without moments of anxiety. His wife, understandably, was very concerned about his health. She was convinced that the procedure of donating bone marrow wouldn't be in his best interest. She was always finding research facts to support her claims. To understand the procedure in its old form was frightening. Therefore, she took great interest in the proceedings.

However, this all shifted to a more positive outlook when I went to Fair View Comprehensive Cancer Center on September 25. The stem cell transplant was revealed to me. Some of the doubts were alleviated by a very smart bone marrow stem cell coordinator, Darlene Christian. She was knowledgeable, convincing, and charming. She was Hispanic., short and fair complexion. Darlene was bubbly. She 'd make you laugh when you were in her present. She was a winsome character. Therefore, she talked my brother into participating in the stem cell procedure, the dreaded Bone Marrow Transplant. Perhaps the most crucial statement made was, "Suppose it were you? Wouldn't you want him to help you?"

He answered in the affirmative. So. in a few short weeks, she worked tirelessly on my case to complete the paperwork. An oversized documented file was sent to my insurance company. Correspondence to my brother and I through e-mail and telephone calls were also put in motion.

8

SO, AFTER SURMOUNTING ALL THE difficulties and discouragement life had to throw at him, my brother Neville arrived in town on Sunday, October 19, on a mission of immense proportion. He is five years older than I'm. He's muscular, fairer, and has a full head of dark hair sprinkled with a few grays and he carry a distinguished mustache. At five feet nine inches, he is three inches taller than I am, but he weighs approximately 23 pounds more.

Neville displays the personality of a very amiable guy. He always had a sense of humor that tickles others into laughing. You couldn't have a dull moment in his presence. He always had a story or joke to tell that you have never heard before.

Other than that, Neville lives a very simple life. He is married to Icy and has three very bright and intelligent children, one girl and two boys. The girl and one boy are architects and the other a computer tech. They have all graduated from well-established universities and are all gainfully employed.

Dad as his children refer to him, loves gardening. He cultivates a variety of vegetables, drove a simple car to and from a Public Warehouse. There he worked diligently, with great responsibility, as a forklift driver who controls delivery and acceptance of thousands of pounds of foodstuff each day.

Yet, from his busy schedule he was permitted to take leave and arrived in town to uplift my spirit with great expectation. He was on an on-time, one-of-a-kind, oriented business mission.

Driven by my friend and Elder Patrick Folks, he wasted little time, but moved into action the very next day. Folks was an elder in my church, a business man who runs a couple of restaurants. He is a former military drill sergeant who retired with distinction. He was very kind and helpful to choose to transport Neville. He was ushered into the renowned life-saving center of Fair View Comprehensive Cancer Center. The express purpose of this visit was to present himself for an evaluation.

Subsequently, the first request was for him to surrender some blood for testing. He also submitted to an EKG, urine analysis, and chest X-ray. Additionally, he'd consultations with Dr. Broderick and Dr. Leonard, the oncologists in charge of my case. Dr. Broderick is an Athenian. He speaks Greek and English. He is a very big tall fellow weighing about three hundred pounds. He is fair and very jovial. He speaks in a distinctive fine and polished voice. He has wide experience in Hematology and Oncology. He is Management of relapsed leukemias, lymphomas and myelomas. Prevention and management of Graft versus Host Disease and Conditioning chemotherapy before stem cell transplants were in his field of specialty.

Dr. Leonard was there to support but he was not directly involved in my case, except for consultation purposes. He was much older than his colleague. They declared that Neville had passed the fitness test. He was ready. As a result, we signed the consent for the procedure, and he was ready for the procedures.

The oncologist reiterated, to my brother "You are healthy, Mr. Harding. You are in good shape." Plus, he was the perfect 10/10 that matched up with me. We were the exact blood type. Subject to his medical health qualification to donate stem cells, he was scheduled to receive five doses of Neupogen injection October 31, to raise his white blood cell count on or about. Neupogen works by stimulating the bone marrow to increase the production of white blood cells. It is a clear liquid that is usually given as a shot in an injection. On November 4, the stem cells were to be extracted. Neville sat in the waiting area and played with the ring on his finger. He crossed his legs. He smacked his lips with his tongue as I waited with bathed breath to hear the final verdict.

He was scheduled for the Neupogen injection. This injection was a simple procedure. It was injected in one of two places, either the fleshy upper part of the shoulder or on the upper part of the buttocks. This results in a slight burn. I know, because I've had several, when my counts work stubbornly and failed to rebound. Since my platelets counts were below the standard count level for a catheter implant, 54,000/µL, I'd to receive platelet transfusion before the implant. This was more than a drama.

I arrived at Fair View and went into the lab at 1:30 p.m. Five nurses converged in the room. Each one tried unsuccessfully to identify a suitable vein in my arm to, start an IV, to administer the platelet transfusion. To compound the situation, my blood pressure rose-up to 210/107. From all five trials, not one drop of blood bled from my view. This made the nurses very uncomfortable, but not alarmed. STOP I remained calm, since I'd been through similar situations like these, several times in the recent weeks before this appointment. Therefore, the decision was decisively made to end their unsuccessful efforts and send me to the emergency radiology lab. There expert guidance of equipped technicians could complete the process.

That visit was very productive. I was made very comfortable, although the lab was deathly cold. The tech was a young Hispanic man. He was slim built, average height and very fair. He wrapped my shivering body with warm blankets, then he performed the procedure. Its alternative, risks, and possible complications were discussed with me. After informing me, I signed the consent, evidenced by my signature. I was placed in a supine position on the table, followed by the tech's taking of scout images of my chest. Further, he prepared and draped me in a sterile fashion, at the right side of my neck and upper chest. He administered, sedation and the catheter procedure began.

"A catheter, also called a port (or Port-A-Cath), a small medical appliance, that is installed beneath the skin. It connects the port to a vein. under the skin. The port has a septum through which drugs can be injected and blood samples drawn many times. Usually, this means less discomfort for the patient than a more typical needle stick."

Guided by the aid of ultrasound technology, the twenty-seven-centimeter tube was tunneled into the right internal jugular vein after the application the of anesthetic. For safety, only local anesthetic was applied, because I'd eaten a sandwich before the procedure. With intravenous anesthetic, it could induce vomiting, and that could be counterproductive. The catheter hung from the right side of my chest, about three inches below the clavicle, or collar bone, leaving my hands free.

It hung in three knots, with identifiable color-coded port which hung from the catheter. Each one was specifically employed during transfusion and was drawing blood. Special care had to be given to keep the catheter clean. Like an IV line, it was very susceptible to transmitting and contracting infection when it was wet. As a result, when I bathed, I followed a similar method of protection and covered it with plastic wrapping. The nurses shared similar stories like I heard at Palm Hospital of patients who carelessly immersed the catheter in water and it caused them to die, as a result, of infection.

Therefore; of all this preparation, on October 28, I was admitted to the fourth floor of the Fair View Comprehensive Cancer Center. This was the location of the is the bone marrow stem cell department. Two days later, I started preparation to receive chemotherapy. I was attached to an IV pole and had saline pumped into my veins through the catheter to hydrate my body. This was to set me on the road to fulfill my date with destiny, stem cell transplant, on November 4. This would be the culmination of all the preparation and drama leading up to that day.

Accordingly, as planned, I was subjected to a rigorous regimen of chemotherapy for the next five days. Each dose was done intravenously given. From all accounts; these procedures should have caused serious consequences. This, I was told, was inevitable. So, I braced myself for the impact. I would fight fire with fire. I stood on the unshakable Word of God, like the Word in Nahum 1:9, which tells me, *"This affliction would not comeback,"* and Isaiah 53:5, *"But he was wounded for our transgression, he was bruised for our iniquities: the chastisement of our peace was upon him; and by his stripes we are healed."* Therefore, I prayed against every evil attack of side effects. "They won't come upon me," I declared. Accordingly, I proved the Word of God to be trustworthy.

As a matter of fact, the nurse coordinator for the Bone Marrow Transplant, Unit told me: "The procedure of chemotherapy with the transplant is going to kick your butt." Yet, perhaps, she did not realize that I had an eternal perspective of the total procedure My healing had already taken place in the heavenly realms. Therefore, I simply said in my mind "We'll see," because I'd just witnessed the miraculous hand of God in the radiology lab.

The fact was that I prayed simply, "God, please don't let me bleed." I didn't specify when this should be because there were two occasions for this to happen, and one prayer took care of both. So, when the nurses tried to find a vein to administer platelet transfusion and stuck me five times, each one supported the same verdict: "You are dried as a peach." For each stick, the needle came out without a speck of blood on the point. It was that simple.

Similarly, when the radiology lab technician completed his procedures, both for platelet transfusion and the catheter implant, he had a similar result manifested. After the task, I asked him, "How much did I bleed?" and he said, "You didn't bleed." This was miraculous, because a little bleeding always happens during a catheter implant.

For this reason, the same God rho protected me in these procedures, won't he do the same when the transplant took place? You bet he would. Thus, I became brave and self-assured as I waited for the chemotherapy to take effect. This process, known as conditioning, was expected to cause me to suffer seriously. Some or a combination of the following side effects would affect me: nausea and vomiting, diarrhea, hair loss, mouth sores, dry mouth, and perhaps swelling of the parotid glands located in my cheek, plus dehydration and mucousitis (mouth sore). Also, symptoms of swelling and discomfort for several hours could occur during posttransplant. These could last for twenty-four to seventy-two hours. There could be memory loss, fatigue, numbness, tingling of the extremities, and several other side effects. It would be safe to say that I lost my hair about two weeks after the procedure. Frankly, some of the other symptoms were present but didn't affect me adversely. What affected me was nausea and anorexia, (loss of appetite). I hardly rested in bed. Sometimes I sat up for the entire day.

Then, I was given a day of rest after this conditioning period, which ushered me into the big day, transplant day, or day zero. I was pregnant with desire. I experienced nervous knots in my stomach. Every day after, would be named day plus 1, day plus 2, day plus 3, and so on.

On day zero, the nurse, Sandra, prepared me for the transplant. This was supposed to be a big thing. Benadryl and Tylenol were administered to me in tablet form. Preparation time took approximately thirty to forty minutes. One other nurse, Emelia, had to witness the start of the procedure. To the joy of my heart, Sandra, suggested that we pray and sought God's intervention. The trio, symbolizing the Father, the Son, and the Holy Ghost, laid hands on the cold plastic container of plasma and offered it to God as a gift for my total healing. I was given the privilege of praying. I asked God to allow the contents of the package to do what it was supposed to do without the side effects. This was, indeed, to fulfill the prayer and prophecy made by my fellow elder at Fire Worship Center on that Sunday, after church, in February

2014: "Lord give my brother a new bone marrow." Then in humility, {lay supine on my bed and submitted to the three hours of a patient's no-turning-back journey.

The procedure was incident-free. I didn't try to think or reason about anything. While I tried to relax and distance my mind from what was happening, but I couldn't. Also, I couldn't pray anymore, nor could I speak. I just lay in the presence of God, knowing that his words say: *"In the same way, the Spirit helps us in our weakness. We do not know what we ought to pray for, but the Spirit himself intercedes for us through wordless groans. 27 And he who searches our hearts knows the mind of the Spirit, because the Spirit intercedes for God's people in accordance with the will of God"* The bag of life-giving plasma was hung on the IV pole, and it was infused into my veins just like when I was given platelet transfusion. I watched a Miami basketball team won their game between bouts of sleep. I didn't realize when the procedure 'was completed. I didn't have any unusual feeling, except that I couldn't fall asleep. That necessitated a sleep aid to break the cycle. I woke up during the night, went to the restroom several times, and spent the rest of the night sitting up, reading and mediating.

I was glad to see the sun rise the next day. My window facing the east gave full advantage of watching the rise of the early-morning sun and the birth of a brand-new day. I felt a great sense of relief and was rather surprised that the procedure was so simple.

The days following the transplant were also incident-free. I didn't have nausea or vomiting. I had no chest pain or tightness. There were no heart rate or blood pressure changes. As a matter of fact, my blood pressure remained normal throughout, like 116/66. I had very little loose stool, no diarrhea or cramping; no fever, chills, or flushing; and no rash or hives. The biggest disadvantage I had, was anorexia (loss of appetite) and weakness. I was quite weak for a few days. Then, suddenly I felt stronger. My platelet count "shot up", and I was fooled into believing that it was going to remain that way. I began walking and running. I was elated. I lived with low blood platelet count for months and now I finally got over this. However, as quickly as it rose it tumbled again. I flopped like a banana leaf hug over a flame. I'd to get shots of Neupogen through platelet transfusion a couple of times.

Then, the real weakness blew my mind. It became a reality. I had sustained a full bout of anorexia and fatigue that I had never experienced before. I was getting along so well with eating small portions, until one day I ate something that turned my stomach upside down and I vomited. This created the passage of the worst anorexic feeling. It lasted for weeks. Even when I was discharged it continued. Slowly, at a snail's pace, my appetite began to increase. I'd a roller-coaster ride with eating for months afterward.

Before I got there, though, each day the doctors came to check on me and marveled at my recovery. Recovery time for the average leukemia patient, older and younger, who received a transplant, was about twenty-one to thirty days. I had my procedure November 4 and was released November 20. That was a mere sixteen days. For sixty- eight years old, that was very good. That was remarkably quick for transplant recovery. I was up and walking the hallways and exercising. I wanted to get out, so I did everything extra. When I was strong enough to walk properly, I practically ran.

When I was in Palm Hospital, the oncologist gave me three instructions: stay out of the bed, wash my hands, and walk. So, I did. My church brother Delroy, left work during his lunchtime to come and walk with me up and down the hall. Soon I was walking so fast that visitors who came to see me couldn't keep pace with me. Therefore, I employed the same effort at Fair View.

Probably, the most interesting feature of this transformational process was displayed by the donor, my brother Neville. He unselfishly lay on his back for six hours during the harvesting of his stem cells. This was more than a sacrifice. Perhaps the most amazing thing was that he was seventy-two years old, one of if not the oldest male ever to donate stem cells. He went through this ordeal incident-free and in the best of spirits. The average age considered for donation is eighteen to age sixty in Western medical records. This age sixty was erased and replaced by age seventy-two. He was the best donor with whom they had ever worked, the technician said. "Oh yes, he has perfect veins," he had remarked on the day as he harvested the stem cells.

To make experience even more meaningful, my brother's willingness and heartfelt satisfaction gave pleasure in not only this role, but also those who supervised the process. Certainly, he had served a cause bigger and greater than himself, *A Wrinkle in Time*. Nothing deters a good man from doing what is honorable). Yes, he's a very good man. Because he was serving this cause, the six hours he spent on his back, giving up six million cells with absolutely reflected no reservation. His dear wife, Icy had stood by his side, giving moral and spiritual support.

This had to have been more significant than just a job well done. There had to be of necessity, a more divine meaning to this remarkable strength and courage. Therefore, from my reflection, I realized that my brother had an eternal perspective of the whole situation. He had been focused upon the promise of giving me a better life, rather than on the problems and difficulties it would cost to fulfill this self-assumed mandate. He had felt discomfort. He had felt tired from lying six hours without the freedom to move about, but he had known that his effort would materialize into the beautiful reality of seeing me regain my health. He knew that "*all things work together for good to them that love God, to them who are the called according to his purpose,*" like (Romans 8:38 KJV) says.

Therefore, I began to ask the Lord questions. I needed answers to substantiate my conjecture. There had to be a cause more compelling. There is the dignity and profundity of devotion and there is the beauty and responsibility to God's eternal plan. As it turned out, there was indeed a more.

There was more than meet the eye. There was a bigger picture, captured on the tapestry of eternal perspective, the story that had to be told. For God to appoint unto them that mourn in Zion, to give unto them beauty for ashes, the oil of joy for mourning, the garment of praise for the spirit of heaviness; that they might be called trees of righteousness, the planting of the LORD, that he might be glorified." And as Nev. offered up his sacrifice, glorifying the Lord, he made history. His story had to be written. Therefore, Derrick could not die with this word in him unfilled.

Unmistakably, the most intriguing aspect to this incredible act of courage and unselfish spiritual engagement was yet to be told. This had validated my conjecture. For one thing, whereas Neville spent six hours on his back, listening to the silent effusion as the motion of the machine responded while it extracted his blood, Jesus, the son of God, spent six hours on the cross listening, as public sentiments changed against him. He was not whom they thought He was. They chose Barabbas and called for Jesus' blood. He was suspended between earth and heaven. His Father allowed Him to listen to the distasteful ridicule of a faithless crowd.

My brother made provision for me to get the five million cells that I needed. He started giving his blood at 9:00 a.m. and finished approximately 3:00 p.m., six hours. He arose and walked to my room, smiling. This was something Jesus didn't give himself the chance to do. He was hung on the cross also from 9:00 a.m. to3:00 p.m., Then at 3:00 p.m., he cried out "It is finished!" *I should have been crucified, I should have suffered and died, I should have hung on the cross in disgrace, but Jesus God's Son took my place."* He didn't have the chance to walk off the cross and smile. This reminds me of the song:

> *I had a debt I could not pay*
> *He paid a debt He did not owe*
> *I needed someone to wash my sins away*
> *And now I sing a brand -new song*

> *"Amazing Grace, all day long,*
> *Christ" Jesus paid a debt*
> *that I could never pay.*

Whereas my brother's smile confirmed victory over the flesh and human struggles, Jesus' cries from His ordeal declared victory for mankind over sin and death. He didn't step down from the cross. He cut down like a butchered animal, that involuntarily submitted to death. It was for this cause that He came and for this cause that He died. It was for a less similar cause that my brother submitted to his ordeal, to see and hear his brother's litany, spoken against fear, not lamenting in despair. Jesus spoke the words that drew salvation's plan. *"Amazing grace how sweet the sound, the sweet song pended, that saved a wretch like me, I once was lost but now I'm found, was blind but now I see."*

His words tore the curtain of the temple in Jerusalem, from top to bottom, that separated man from God. "Now man can come boldly before His throne of grace, that we may obtain mercy and find grace, to help us in time of need." (Hebrews 4:16 KJV)

My brother gave me the chance to live until I am one hundred and twenty years old, to fulfil the mandate in Genesis 6:3: *My spirit shall not abide in man forever, for he is flesh, his days shall be one hundred and twenty years.* Jesus death and resurrection gave me life eternal. I regained all the zest, confidence energy, the devil sapped from my body. I built a new immune system and retook all the childhood inoculations to fight against diseases. Since then no trace of Leukemia has been found in my body.

Jesus' blood transformed the immune system of man's sinful nature, as He gave His life as ransom for all, that we may have abundant life. As they cut Him down from the cross; His limp body must have wobbled. Joseph of Arimathea a secret follower, of Christ, wrapped His wounded body for burial. My brother was not buried. but Jesus was, so that He could rise again to fulfill the scripture: "He rose on the third day."

I didn't rise from the dead because I didn't die. However, I received new life from that transplant. I was filled with hope and expectation. One day, I tested my strength as I walked up and down the hallway during recovery. On that day of my sixteen days after the transplant, I struggled in my quest to regain strength. I stumbled like a drunkard, but I did manage to keep my balance. To my utter surprise, a nurse sympathetic to my cause, gave me a chair on wheels, to push, walk and balance myself. That however, would've detracted from my walk to strengthen my body. I started, but I refused it, and by sheer willpower buttressed by the courage of the Holy Spirit, I plodded on.

Another day, the most remarkable thing took place during one of my walks. As I struggled and stumbled on the way, I kept meditating on the Word of God on to the word that is a lamp unto my feet and a light to my path. Suddenly, I felt a warm hand around me. I knew instantly whose hand it was. It was a young nursing assistant that accepted salvation as I led him to the Lord two nights before. I turned my head to him and said "thanks," and the Holy Spirit warmed my heart.

In response, he just said, "I'm listening." This young nursing assistant was kind and compassionate. He was the first to answer my call when I alerted the nursing station. His advice was sound. He would tell me, "Don't push yourself too hard, Derrick. Take it one day at a time." Whenever he came to work, he stuck his head through my door and asked, "Derrick, my friend, are you all right? Can I bring you anything, some tea or water?" If I said yes, his response was, "Coming right up."

Likewise, in those very critical moments, the doctors arrived, looking smart, experienced, knowledgeable, and businesslike, were ready to alleviate any signs of fears. Therefore, they and the efficient nursing staff displayed themselves in an efficacious manner. The nurses, my first line of contact, were most polite and seemingly good-natured. They aimed at making the remaining portion of my stay pleasant, as a home away from home. They weren't short of encouraging and comforting words. They always spoke positive words to uplift my confidence. I rarely made a call that wasn't answered immediately.

My generous nature harkened to the profundity of their kindness and willingness to do their job well. Hence, I showed my appreciation to them as I wrote thank-you notes to them on my personal business card as I did at Palm Hospital. Not finding adequate words on my own, I turned to the scriptures help. Therefore, I quoted a verse from 3 John 1: "Beloved I wish above all things that you may prosper and be in health as your soul prospers." Everyone was very thrilled to receive this token. One said she would wear it as a badge. Others said they would read it every day. One doctor stuck his on the bulletin board for all to see.

Indeed, all I can sing is
"Just for me, just for me
Jesus came and did it just for me.
Donnie McClain

9

THEN CAME THE DAY OF reckoning. It was day plus 16. I awoke from a long sleepless night of anxious tossing and turning. When I opened my eyes, I couldn't concentrate on reading because I was too fatigued from lack of sleep. My eyes felt very uncomfortable, as though a foreign matter was rolling in them. They were watery and red, yet my focus was firmly set on going home. There was no cloud to dim the light of my silver lining. All the semblance of distraction paled in comparison to the joy and anticipation that comforted me in these troubled uncertain moments.

Indeed, I contemplated the word "weeping may endure for a night, but joy comes in the morning." Psalm 30:5 This was the day when Dr. Obandu and his team would make the decision that I was ready to assume the next phase of my journey to recovery. Dr. Obandu, was an Indian. He was thin bodied, slightly dark and had streaks of gray in his hair. He was the leader of a most effective and compassionate medical team. Therefore, at 5:00 a.m., the thick fog hovering over the November morning, caused no distraction. I took off my gown, wrapped my catheter area in plastic, and took a quick bath. God forgave what I did. I'm sure, that if it were put to the test, I would've failed outright, but water did touch some parts of my skin away from the plastic wrap.

I tried to have devotions, but I failed to *concentrate.* I was anxious for everything. Therefore, I struggled to make my request known, but I'm sure that I'd say some things. However, to fill this void, I wrote a journal entry while I sat on the long -cushioned bench by the window. At times, my hand shook while I wrote as the thoughts of as what-if popped upon in my mind faster than I could write them down.

By 6:30 a.m., the sunlight's indispensable strength imposed its dominance and rested the early-morning fog. The temperature was seventy-three degrees Fahrenheit high and sixty-six below. I sat at the window and admired the persistency of the powerful sunlight as it slowly and deliberately imposed its will. In-deed it relieved the morning of its coat of gloom and replaced it with its brightness.

The branches of the American oak below my window stilled their movement in the almost- windless morning. The smaller oaks around it patterned its example. Droplets of water on the leaves of the topmost branches, blessed by the sunlight, fashioned a design of perfect tapestry. A nightingale chose to upset the balance by hopping from branch to branch, f lapping its wings and shaking off the water. This created a more magnificent spectrum during its improvised bath, symbolizing the unmistakable interdependence of nature.

Below the trees stood five feet tall by five feet wide orange umbrella awnings. There were black cast iron tables and matching chairs, waiting for some leisurely patients to entertain their visitors later. To the east, one of the tall, stately structures of Fair View Hospital towered over the face of the picturesque scene. A short distance from the hospital, I could see and hear man's transit design, the Tri-Rail train. It was easing back and forth, up and down the rail, powered by its no driver electric engine, as it traveled to and from southern parts of the state. Yet I waited for that decisive hour to come.

By eight o'clock, the sun was shining gorgeously in my room. It brought warmth that was very comforting. Then I heard a rap on my door, but I was disappointed. That was breakfast time. The traveling waiter knew that I wasn't eating. I'd absolutely no appetite. Nonetheless, she asked out of courtesy, "what would like to eat?" The conclusion was known even before I answered. I wouldn't eat anything. So, I answered, "Give me some tea. Thank you."

In response, I just took a couple of sips and put away the cup. Soon lunch would come; and it made space limited. The breakfast tray would be shuffled aside but not removed, and dinner, accordingly, would find no place. Therefore, all trays would be removed late in the afternoon.

The only comfort I found, was to enjoy the challenges of moving up and down the hallway on my walks and adventures. Every day I would always discover something new, exciting or challenging. Most of the time, especially mornings and evenings, I'd had the support of the nurses, who admired my tenacity and determination. There was always somebody on hand to say an encouraging word.

However, at ten o'clock, that special morning, the decisive hour came. The chief oncologist Dr. D Obandu, ushered his team into my room to herald the gladsome tidings. They didn't come to distribute goodies but to relieve my expectant heart. The joy of my heart was about to spill over from excitement, nervousness, and understandable expectation.

The Oncologist led me through the usual questions. "Do you have diarrhea, vomiting, headaches, burning in your eyes, or feeling any pain?" He squeezed my abdomen. "Hold up your shirt. He has no rash and no swelling of the lymph nodes. How about fever, any chills since yesterday?"

"No," I replied.

He listened to my lungs. "Breathe in and out deeply. Lungs are clear. Now breathe normally," As he listened to my heart, he confirmed, "His heart is good." He turned to the team. "I think he is ready to go."

I watched my face in the mirror, and it had a pleasant countenance. The team all gave the affirmative nod. Some members answered, "Yes, he is ready." The members of the team shook my hand.

"Congratulations. We think you have done well. You need to be careful now," the chief cautioned. "The nurse will give further instructions at your release."

When will my appetite come back?" I asked.

"I can't give you a definite answer, but we can assure you that it will gradually come back," he replied.

At that moment, I remembered the song my wife and I sang the first night on our way to Palm Hospital:

> *Jesus took my burden, I could no longer bear, Jesus took my burden in answer to my prayer;*
> *My anxious fear subsided, my spirit was made strong;*
> *Jesus took my burden and he left me with a song.*

Oh, I was so overwhelmed with emotion that I cried unrestrained. The team closed the door and left quietly. My anxious fears had subsided, and my spirit was made strong. In my lonely hours God gave me blessed consolation. He told me He was there to make me strong. Through it all I learned to trust in Jesus.

I cried myself to sleep. When I wake, I watched television. It was my longest but most meaningful day at Fair View. Within the tedious days of frustration, times of anxiety and discomfort, I finally saw a light at the end of the proverbial tunnel. It was a light of mixed blessings.

At 4:00 p.m., my wife, Shelly, came to take me home, but the paperwork was incomplete. She boosted my confidence and we passed the time in conversation, though she was not happy that I invited her to come so early. What could one expect? I just wanted to go home. However, with her there, I was relieved of the anxiety.

I relaxed, and we found lighthearted things to occupy our minds until the nurse brought the paperwork.

She read over the instructions, which included the summary of my hospitalization, packaged in a twenty-two-page booklet. It highlighted physicians who cared for me, plus allergies I suffered, and medications applied in my case. Likewise, the nurse discussed not only the medications to be taken as a follow-up but also the administration procedures.

The booklet, packed with information, delineated and described the disease in simple and layman's language for my Care Giver who would further explain things. She was Pauline, my wife's sister. She was indeed a tower of strength to me. I tip my proverbial hat to her. She was genuine. She came November 25, and she left in the middle of January.

Imagine, though, you ask her to fix something for you to eat, and when you receive it, it was unpalatable because of the anorexia I was experiencing. After she put all her love, care, and effort to work, it must have been discouraging when I could not eat it. This was not very nice.

Then, explanation of the exit document, was a very tedious understand, but it was rendered possible by my tremendous expertise of my caregiver. When she came, I was helpless. I couldn't take off my shirt. I could hardly bend to put on my shoes. That was a task that left me winded after ten minutes effort. I'd a difficult time taking a shower, especially during November to January. It was a problem to avoid soaking the catheter. Additionally, I'd to wear thick clothing even in the house and when go to bed. I'd a difficult time falling asleep and I would wake up in the night shivering from cold. Where ever I went, I'd to wear a mask and latex gloves to protect myself.

At one time, I found myself taking more than fifty-one tablets during the month of November to January, but not on a regular basis. These were my oncologist recommendation. This was disconcerting at times. Sometimes my indecision discouraged my caregiver. She frowned at me a couple of times, but she stuck with me and saw me through the roughest part of my sickness. After her departure, I quickly adjusted to my wife's care.

Every morning, she'd put out my medication, but I assumed the role of making that ginger and lemon tea to "warm up the tank" as my wellness physician jokingly said. I learned the combination of the medication, so we took turn in making sure that the preparations were administered. If time didn't allow her to do so, then I'd take the responsibility. Everything was written out for easy access.

As a result, my health continued to be stabilize in the sense that my counts didn't fall dramatically, nor did they rise rapidly. My platelets bordered between 55 and 70/µL, while my hemoglobin showed calibrated readings that were within the region of 9.5 to 10 g/Dl. My white blood cells remeasured 3.1 to 3.3/µL. Yet, my oncologist gave me positive reviews because I was absent of other symptoms.

Gradually, he withdrew me from the transplant medication but left one, acyclovir 800, mg tablets, which is used to treat infections caused by certain types of viruses. "It treats cold sores around the mouth (caused by herpes simplex), shingles (caused by herpes zoster), and chicken pox. This medication is also used to treat outbreaks of genital herpes. In people with frequent outbreaks, acyclovir helps to reduce the number of future episodes. This medication may also help reduce how long pain remains after the sores heal. In addition, in people with a weakened immune system, acyclovir can decrease the risk of the virus spreading to other parts of the body and causing serious infections (webmd.com/drugs/2/drug-941/acyclovir-oral/details). I took this medication from transplant date, November 4, 2014, until nine months after. At first, I started on this for a ten-day period, taking one tablet by mouth two times daily, but later, I was instructed to continue it for an extended period, taking three tablets daily.

Obviously, my health recovery didn't follow a lineal pattern but rather cyclical path. Therefore, I've had small setbacks along the way. Science says Graft-versus-host had been the culprit. I've had infections in my mouth and my eyes for months that stubbornly wouldn't go away. First, the symptoms started in my mouth, in which I discovered white patches that burned when I ate spicy food or drink hot beverage or soup. My oncologist told me that I'd contracted the graft-versus-host disease (GVH), which I am denying. God expects me to live abundant life. It is illegal for this disease to take residence in my body. Doctor says it came about because my immune system was resisting my donor's immune system. This contradictory to the word of God. Research says the older the donor was, the more likely it was for the host to be infected, and my donor at 72 years old set the record for being the oldest male to have successfully donated stem-cell. That means I am on the side of History. I am the first person to be healed from stem cell issued from the oldest person who made donation. Similarly, Doctors are confused that there is no cure for GVH, but they have me as their guinea pig. I am on the side of History, the first person in the world to be healed of the symptoms of this disease.

Secretly and publicly I am partaking in the Devine nature of the Lord and Savior Jesus Christ. (2ndPeter3-4) According to His divine power He has given me all things pertain to life and godliness through the *knowledge* of Him who has called me to glory and virtue. He has given me exceeding great and precious promises so by these exceeding great and precious promises, I partake in His Divine plan. "This is a love of unmerited favor. It is a love that is offered to all of mankind through God's grace. God's divine nature is also the source of righteousness in the world."

My oncologist, bless his heart, for his effort, he recommended dexamethasone 0.5 mL to swish and spit for ten days when I had mouth sores. I'd take 5 mL in my mouth, swish it for ten minutes, and spit it out. This I gladly put in effect, and I anticipated good results. After ten days, the symptoms seemed to require more rigorous treatment. Therefore, the oncologist smiled and demonstrated his positive tone. "I got your back Derrick he said lightheartedly,

"Okay, I know what to do. You need tacrolimus ointment 0.1 percent. You will anoint the spots in your mouth four times per day for ten days. This will clear it up." Yet, ten days had come and gone, and I've had several refills, but GVH was still trying to impose its will and hold me hostage. It insists on robbing me of the manifested total health that was promised to me. After 6 months, though, I was withdrawn from this medication. Bless the Lord.

However, it hid behind the scenes and made another showing, this time, of all the places, in my eyes. It caused burns and itches and, together with the medication, produced dry eyes, which became very disturbing. Dry eye syndrome is caused by a chronic lack of sufficient lubrication and moisture on the surface of the eye. Dr. Richard A. Adler, member of the All about Vision Editorial Advisory Board, states that dry eyes range from subtle but constant eye irritation to significant inflammation and even scarring of the front surface of the eye. In addition, to being called dry eye syndrome, it was also called conjunctivitis and dry eye disease.

Because there were less tears in my eyes, I found that when I expressed the emotion of crying, no tears f lowed. But on January 17, at 3:45 a.m., I found myself praying in the wee hours of the morning. Among other things, I cried out to my master for the return of my tears. As I prayed, I closed my eyes tight, and I felt tears streaming from my eyes. I got out of bed and went to the mirror in my bathroom to confirm if they were real. True enough, tears had wet my face. This means that the conjunctivitis is only a name and "At the name of Jesus every knee shall bow", Therefore, if Leukemia bowed, GVH bowed so will conjunctivitis. So, I sat up pen these words I called sweet tears.

Sweet Tears

Oh, how sweet are the tears that flow, down from my eyes,
so parched I know, their trickling streams unhurriedly
flow,
They popped in my ears and show each drop so rich, so
pristine pure; warm to the touch, and soothing to the eyes.
I still remember, their slain taste, O, that my tears will
forever flow. Derrick Harding

Notwithstanding, the above discomforts, graft-versus-host was determined to get me one way or the other. Therefore, in addition to all its vicious consequences, the problem was compounded by effects of scleroderma, which caused inflammation to cover certain muscles in my body. While the symptoms manifested themselves mostly in my arms and legs, they seemed to reveal themselves over my whole body. I felt pain and stiffness in the area below and around the area of my armpit, but the manifested symptoms included swelling, pain, and stiffness of my left arm, from my shoulder to the wrist. It curtailed my range of movement, especially raising my hands above my head. Yet I am denying that rascal, of a Devil.

From all accounts, though, the prognosis seemed to be good, not just from the doctor's point of view but from the portals o heaven. Prednisone 50 mg was the recommended treatment, which I took on reducing value, from one tablet a day for ten days, to one-half for another ten days. This was resisting its progress. In addition, my oncologist recommended alendronate sodium 70 mg to counteract the effects of osteoporosis that could occur.

Apart from my personal physical issues, I suffered unfairly in terms of my professional position. IT was this sickness that curtailed my working hours. I anticipated that I would have resumed after a few short months, but I didn't understand the nature of the disease. The wider circle of my professional association such as the Teachers' Union expected me to resume as early as possible, but the inner circle of my school was not ready to receive me and didn't make provision to accommodate me. I couldn't resume my former job, because I was on medical leave for more than one year. According to the school board's policy, in such an instance, I would've to be surplus, that is, I was put on a list, and the board found me another place at another school if there were no vacancies at my former school.

Things didn't go right from the start. I chose to apply to other schools to find a suitable position not wanting wait on the Board to place me. Having written more than a dozen applications, I came up short of finding a job. However, not being completely well and being anxious I didn't exercise faith. At the last minute however, just before the opening of school, I got two offers. The first was much too far to travel, since I was just getting back to normal routine of driving on the road, though the position was in a B grade school. I turned it down, and for some strange reason, I accepted one in an inner-city school nearer to my home. This turned out to be a nightmare.

It so happened that this inner-city school was like no other in which I ever taught. I never imagined that such a school ever exists in twenty first century America. The whole atmosphere of the school and the changing face of the duties I had to perform made me nervous and always kept my blood pressure way above normal.

Eighty five percent of the students exhibited some form of deviant behavior on a regular basis, including truancy, fighting, or poor academic performance. This school was widely publicized in the news with incidents of students being arrested for carrying loaded guns in school bag.

One of the classes I was assigned to was on the Superintendent's watch list. Their grades and behavior were closely monitored. The helper that was assigned to the classes would pull out a few of the worse behaved students to teach, but that, presented a conflict of who to go and who to stay. Plus, those left behind, just naturally sparked problems. I've witnessed half a dozen big fights. Students curse obscene words as if they couldn't express themselves any other way.

To make matters worse, the school board chief declared a bold proposal to reduce suspension and expulsion, which were, the most effective way of dealing with discipline. Students were sent to an alternate education program, which couldn't accommodate them because of space. When a student misbehaved, he was written up and sent to the administrator he in turn sent him or her off to this program. The student returned to the teaching environment worse than before because he or she knew that no serious consequence was offered.

In this atmosphere, I found it difficult to manage discipline in regular classes. Students rolled up assignments and used the paper to them to stone each other as they do with the pencils. One boy climbed on the filing cabinet to do a dance. The class break out in cheers. Somebody turned off the light and swore it wasn't him even though I saw him with his hand on the switch. In these cases, you write referrals but find the student get a slap on the wrist, a warning, and he or she is back in class the next period or the following day because of the no-suspension policy.

In the midst, of all this chaos, I was placed on a surplus list again. The attendance at this school was cut in half. Almost a third of the staff withdrew, resigned, or asked for transfer in the first semester, including two coaches. According to the protocol that governs this case, I kept my position, going to school and receiving my salary. Then I was reinstated because another teacher left. This didn't work in my favor. I was replaced in a worse situation than I was in before. The condition drained me. Each evening I was a nervous wreck. I staggered to my car happy to survive another day.

The rest of this is history. I was given a poor evaluation for not being indecisive in controlling discipline, compounded by excessive absences from school for medical reasons. Now I'd to seek special permission to keep medical leave. This was the first in my fifteen years working in the school system that I'd been relegated to poor performance. In my last job before I became ill, the principal's last word to me was "Mr. Harding, you've done a phenomenal job with your students. Your test results show it." Contradictorily, however, when I tried to resume this position on the very day, she hired one of my former students to work on the staff. Of course, she said no position existed in my discipline. The general opinion however is that if she wanted to, she could have made provision to accommodate me.

However, I viewed it as a temporary setback. God, who gave me back a position in the first place, would orchestrate ways for me to succeed. He knew this would've happened. But what I must emphasize is that I could've done well with a few more months' leave. My health conditions seriously militated against my doing well. However, I must confess that I found real favor with the administration, who tried to arrange teaching positions to accommodate me because of health reasons. Yet I must be honest I was barely going through the motion.

Going to school was a chore that left me very exhausted as I said, at the end of each day. I was a total wreck. To make the problem worse, the discipline I worked in was totally changed. There were new standards books and programs to contend with. This school district changed programs like the seasons change yearly. As soon as you get accustomed to teaching a course using a set of strategies, you return to school for the new school year having to learn and adapt to new sets of principles and procedures.

But God must be confident in me, to give me this test, and I'll do my best to pass it. He'll cause me to rise again. I shall rebound, because there is greatness in me. One song writer wrote, *"But I shall rise again, there is no power on earth can tie me down, I shall rise again, and death won't keep down in the ground."* What the devil meant for harm, God is going to turn it around for good.

Perhaps one of the indicators that I should present to confirm the working of God's favor in my life was with regards to my financial operation. Provisions were made through benefits from my employer, Daniel County Schools, which gave each full-time employee a benefit package. Included were the hospital indemnity coverage, short-term disability funds from the Bradford Insurance Company, and a compensation of 60 percent of your salary for twenty-two weeks. Also, I received one month's pay for sick leave through my affiliation with the teachers' union. Through these sources, Jehovah Jarrah provided for me in the most incredible way. It was the first time in my adult life that I had so much money in my bank account. I was never in want, I never borrowed, I never owed anyone, and I made several charitable contributions to my church and to friends in need, and God kept sufficient funds in my basket until I could resume work. When I resumed, I'd just less than $1,000 in my account. Therefore, I needed to hold to an employment.

In addition, there is much to be said about my insurance company, and this is by no means all. But this company gave me royal treatment. At first, because I didn't understand all there was to know, I was very tense, but as the company took care of my business, I became more confident. This was spearheaded by frequent communication. They gave explanation of my benefits and summary of claims for services performed by my doctors. The statement was broken down clearly for me to understand what I need to know on my next claim.

When one of the hospitals and some of their affiliates swamped me with bills, I called my case manager, Samuel Foreman, and he guided me through these difficult periods of sorting things out and relieving me of the imminent stress. My insurance company paid all my bills in full. The company has never asked me to pay out any extra cost. And if I'd to signal one person who championed my cause, Samuel would be my choice. He has been a tower of strength to me. My only regret is that I wasn't introduced to him sooner because of some communication instability between Palm Hospital and the insurance company.

For the seven months I was not registered in the bone marrow stem cell program. However, when he came on board, he literally managed my case with godly wisdom, diligence, and a kind heart. Samuel displayed a good sense of balance of communicating without being overbearing. He didn't tell me what to do. He coached me in a suggestive way. He gave me available options; we discussed them and came up with a plan. We set goals, and I worked toward them. When I accomplished one goal satisfactorily, we set another.

One thing I loved about Samuel was that he was always tender-hearted and empathetic to me. He demonstrated full understanding of my health needs and gave me significant information to manage my illness. He never questioned the position of the physicians but asked me to engage them on merits and demerits of taking one medication as opposed to another. He always sought to make me as comfortable as possible with my doctors, my medication, and my overall recovery. He was a living testimony of the services provided by my insurance company.

Yet, with all the skirmishes of the aftermath of leukemia, there may appear to be some controversy with-regard to my healing. But I can give the assurance that there is absolutely nothing contradictory to be considered. I'll be undaunted. I won't concede any ground to doubts. I won't relinquish hold on the fact that I'm totally healed.

Further, be it resolved: Since God is infallible, then his Word is infallible, or unfailing. That means it's never wrong, and thus it is absolutely- trustworthy and free from error, so reliable that God honors his Word above his name (Psalm 138:2). Likewise, 2 Timothy 3:16–17 says, "*The word of God may thoroughly furnish or equip his servant to do good works.*" Simply, it means "to furnish or equip for service against extenuating circumstances." *Equip* or *furnish* is transitive verb. **A** transitive verb performs an action on an object. For example, *God parted the Red Sea.* (*Red Sea* is the object on which the action took place or is performed upon.) God is the doer who is doing the equipping. He equips for life. This suggests thoroughness or completeness. In other words, God delivers perfection. Perfection is infallible. He heals totally.

Similarly, Psalm 19:7 says, *"The Law of the Lord is perfect, converting or refreshing the soul."* Only a perfect God imputes spiritual perfection. The words of the Lord are pure words, like silver refined in a furnace on the ground, purified seven times- Psalm 12:6 KJV

Jesus is the demonstration of the infallible God. Only He can rest a sinful soul by way of salvation and healing. The scripture in 2nd Corinthians 5:17 says, "Therefore if any man be in Christ, he is a new creature, old things are passed away; behold all things are become new." Consequently, based on the perfect Word from an infallible God, who is omniscient, whose Word never fails, and this is the ground for trusting in God which I would like to propagate: I would like to propose an argument, that God bought us with a price an imperishable seed and, not perishable through His living and abiding word." This word is a seed. When a seed is planted it brings fort fruit of its kind, fruit of healing and righteousness and deliverance that last. "For the grass withers, and the flower falls, but the word of God abides forever. (1 Peter 1:25)

Second, The word shan't return to Him void. So, shall my word be that goes forth out of my mouth: it shall not return unto me void, but it shall accomplish that which I please, and it shall prosper in the thing whereto I sent it. The word of God is sent for my healing. God's word is guaranteed to do what it says it will do. (Isaiah 55:11) Although it tarries it shall come to pass. But He was wounded for our transgressions, he was bruised for our iniquities: the chastisement of our peace was upon him; and with his stripes we are healed. He sent his word and he healed them and delivered them from destruction. He sent His word and healed them (Psalm 107:20). Yet sometimes we must wait if the manifestation is physically delayed, but (Habakkuk 2:3), though the vision-tarries wait for it for it shall come to pass but the word of the Lord remains forever. I stand upon the authority of his Word and declare this thirteenth day of December, at 8:07 p.m., that I, Derrick Harding, am totally healed of leukemia.

Therefore, I'd like to say to the scores of people who can identify with my suffering, that there is hope in Jesus. I offer you hope—not hope to be like me but hope in Christ. The Lord is near to them that are brokenhearted, and He saves those that are humble in spirit. Many are the afflictions of the righteous, but the Lord delivers him out of them all."

Psalm 34:19-20. Your suffering may be different from mine, but it is a struggle nonetheless. You may be sick in body, you may've leukemia or some other cancer or health situation. You may have been dragged over the rugged terrain of adversity, disgraceful treatment and suffering, but I ask you to dream again.

To all those who are suffering with disbelief that hope is not gone, I ask you to dream again. Your dream of healing may be delayed, but you are not denied. Some of you have been praying, some of you have nothing else to do, "Nobody has to teach you how to dream. We're all born dreamers. Somewhere along the line life hits and we stop dreaming. It's time to dream again! God has a plan for our lives, and His plan is bigger than us, so are my ways higher than your ways and my thoughts than your thoughts and heavens are higher than the earth's

So, your God dream should scare you, it should bring you to your knees asking for help. It's time to dream, to live out what God has put in your heart to do. Others are praying for you, but in all your endeavors, I encourage you to put your ultimate faith in God. I encourage you to see yourself walking out of your situation better than you're now." Some of you are Christian, some of you aren't, but God sends rain on the just and on the unjust. Therefore, God doesn't discriminate, the more compelling for you to keep your focus completely on him.

My friends, may I call you friends? I'd like you to know that this message is bigger, much bigger than I'm. I'm manning a task that has great implication, not just for me, but for all those who are furiously engaged in a battle for survival, those who wet their pillow every night with their tears, be it social, physical, emotional, physiological, or spiritual, don't be weary. If you will embrace the message of hope and faith in God, your healing and deliverance are guaranteed.

Your story will take on a new perspective. You'll find out that the Great God who said "Let" and everything in heaven and earth was called into being, God who is so big that he rules the mighty universe, has made himself small enough to live in your heart through the person of Jesus Christ. He'll be as close to you as the very breath you're breathing. He promises not to leave you or forsake you. He'll bring peace and clarity to your mind. This peace and quiet will make you strong, that you can believe that your sickness or your struggle isn't unto death but to give glory to Him. "When you give God the glory, He will write your story" Jeremiah 29:11 says, "*For I know the thought that I have towards you, says the Lord, thoughts of peace and not of evil, to give you an expected end.*" Third John 1 says, "*Beloved, I wish above all things that you may prosper and be in health, as your soul prospers.*" Therefore, when you pass through your deep waters, he *will be* with you, and through the rivers of adversity, they won't over flow you. When you walk through the fire of your broken heart and discomfort, you shall not be burned; neither shall the f lames kindle upon you.

Think of your struggle as deep as the deepest river, the Congo in Africa, it will overflow you even at 850 feet deep, and The Río de la the broadest 137 miles across, none will overpower you. No fire, or life's disaster will affect you. You won't be covered, nor be burned, because Jesus will be with you. When the Children of Israel passed through the red sea Red Sea, a depth of 7,254 feet, (the River Jordan 90 to 100 feet their sandals didn't get wet. When King Nebuchadnezzar heated the furnaces exceedingly and cast Daniel and his companions in it, the king leaped to his feet in amazement and asked his advisers, "Weren't there three men that we tied up and threw into the fire?" They replied, "Certainly, Your

Majesty." Yet there were four seen Daniel 3:24. There was a fourth which puzzled him.

God promised that his word won't return to him unfilled, but it will accomplish that for which he sent it. It'll come to pass. (Isaiah 55:11)

How do I know this? God has done it for me, and he'll do it for you too. I can't guarantee that it will be immediate, nor will it be tomorrow or two weeks from the time you are reading this inspiration, but as sure as night follows day, he will never leave you nor for sake you. November 4, 2018 will be five years since I did my transplant. Though I still have a few issues I never stop dreaming. How do I justify my healing? There has been no trace of Leukemia in my blood. He has done it for me, and he'll do it for you. The Almighty, The undisputed, heavy weight champion of the world, The Alpha, The Omega, The beginning and the end, The Lily of the valley, The Bright and Morning Star, will turn your mourning into dancing. I never stop dreaming, not just for me but for those who are wrestling with the piercing fangs of disease, discouragement, despair, and disappointment, look no further than, (Psalm Healed30:11-12.) He presents a perfect gospel to an imperfect people. I present an imperfect book but a perfect message.

www.ingramcontent.com/pod-product-compliance
Lightning Source LLC
Chambersburg PA
CBHW062019040426
42447CB00010B/2064